The Healthy House Book

The Healthy House Book

Gina Lazenby

THE LYONS PRESS

Published in the US in 2000 by The Lyons Press
First published in 2000 by Conran Octopus Limited

Text copyright © Gina Lazenby 2000
Design and layout copyright © Conran Octopus
Special photography copyright © Conran Octopus

Commissioning editor: Susannah Gough
Senior editor: Emma Clegg
Assistant editor: Lucy Nicholson
Editorial assistant: Lara McCann
Consultant copy editor: Mary Lambert
Proofreaders: Mary Lambert and Colette Campbell
Indexer: Helen Snaith
Americanizer: Lisa Cussans

Design: Lucy Holmes
Picture research: Julia Pashley, Rachel Davies, and Sarah Hopper
Black-and-white photography: Victoria Blackie
Typesetting: Tiger Typeset

Production controllers: Sue Bayliss and Manjit Sihra

ISBN 1-58574-111-6

Library of Congress Cataloging-in-Publication data is available
upon request

Color origination by Sang Choy International, Singapore
Printed in China

Dedication

This book is dedicated to Morel. Thank you for your inspiration
and our home. Without you, and the journey we have shared
together, this book would not have been possible.

Disclaimer

The views expressed in *The Healthy House Book* are the
opinions of the author and are not necessarily endorsed by
the publisher.

CONTENTS

INTRODUCTION

Welcome to *The Healthy House Book*. It is my heartfelt desire that the information in this book will help you to create a better life for yourself and your family. Writing it has been one of the most challenging and inspiring experiences of my life. It took 18 months to create and was the culmination of years of research and personal experience.

The process began at the beginning of the 1990s when I first started to feel unwell. My lifestyle as a company managing director in central London was making me sick, although I couldn't see that at the time. I began to make some improvements to my diet, and I did notice a change. But then a long bout of deep depression followed which forced me to make more drastic changes to my lifestyle. I had been working with a nutritionist for nearly a year when she mentioned that perhaps my home was making me ill. I have to say that, even though I like to think that I have an open mind, I dismissed what she said. However, I did begin to explore this possibility and looked at my home and lifestyle afresh.

My health improved and, as my life progressed, I explored further the deep connection we have with our homes. I became very interested in working with feng shui, and looked at some of the more modern challenges facing us that, perhaps, the first feng shui practitioners in the Far East did not have to consider. I investigated areas such as electromagnetic radiation and chemical pollution, which can have an extremely stressful influence on our homes.

During the last few years I have witnessed people making huge health improvements by focusing on environmental changes, and so I concentrated more on the connection between health and home. In 1997, my partner Morel and I embarked on a major building program for our country home, and this is where the challenges really started as we sought to create a truly healthy home. What we have achieved is a wonderful, peaceful place with a minimum of chemical and electrical pollution. My experience on this subject is therefore very personal.

This book will show you that we all need to make some different choices about our homes and lifestyles if we want to safeguard our health and the health of our families. Doing this effectively is a continuous journey. None of us has all the answers—not even all the experts agree, and opinions about what is right change over time.

The Healthy House Book is therefore based on my opinions and my personal vision, and is not necessarily endorsed by conventional practice or belief. It covers a wide range of subject matter, each with its own specialized researchers and scientists. Although it has been impossible for me to list every attributable source, my hope is that this book will encourage you to dig deeper, to find out for yourself and make your own mind up about the issues that I am raising, and then to adjust your lifestyle according to your own perspective. In short, I hope that *The Healthy House Book* will inspire you.

To support you with the most up-to-date information, advice, and resources for this journey, we have created a website that can expand with the latest research and views on this subject. It can be reached on *www.thehealthyhome.com,* and there you can find answers to your questions, share your own discoveries, and find support from others on the same journey.

Wishing you good luck and good health.

Gina Lazenby

The 20th century gave everyone access to unprecedented and previously unimaginable luxury and convenience. Homes were built with all the modern conveniences that even 50 years ago would have been unthinkable. The time-consuming tasks of food preparation and washing clothes by hand had almost disappeared from the daily household routine. The introduction of convenience foods, vacuum cleaners, washer/dryers, spray cleaners, and no-iron materials meant that, in theory, everyone had more free time than ever before for what is important to each of us. Yet, now, at the beginning of the 21st century, most people complain about the lack of time to do things.

Life has changed very quickly in the last few decades, and our expectations of what we want to achieve have dramatically changed. Information technology via mobile phones, email, and the internet has given all of us the opportunity of immediate communication with anybody, at any time, anywhere on the planet. So it seems odd that with all this high-tech advancement we should still feel stressed and have restricted free time. More and more people are finding that they are cash-rich but time-poor, which means they are unable to enjoy life to the full.

The question is, do our busy lifestyles create problems for us because we have too much to do, or is it because we do not have enough energy to cope? If we explore further and look at why energy levels have become a problem, one reason is that stresses in our environment are, in fact, depleting our emotional and physical resources. As we juggle several projects at any one time, we are aware of how we are using our energy. However, when the source of stress is within our environment it is invisible and unfamiliar, so we do not realize just how much energy we are wasting in dealing with it.

Stress in the home

In the past, very few people considered their homes to be a real source of stress. After all, the home is seen as a place of safety – a sanctuary and retreat. As homes became more cozy and comfortable in the 1980s, particularly with advanced in-home entertainment, people spent more time there. Today, at the start of the 21st century, homes continue to be important because there are many people who want to retreat from the greater pressures in their working environments. Now, more than ever, our homes need to be healthy centers of calm to support and regenerate us, so the idea that they may cause us stress is a revelation. Also our homes are believed to be mirror images of us, so if our homes are suffering, then so are we, physically, mentally, and emotionally.

The fact that our homes can cause stress is not a totally new concept in the West. After World War II, Germany embarked on a huge program of new housing. This boom was followed by the discovery that people who lived in these new homes were starting to suffer from disease and ill health, and a connection was very swiftly made with the construction methods and materials that were being used. It led to the formation of the Bau Biologie movement, which fosters a view that a home is an extension of the human body and that there are various ways of building homes that reconcile modern construction methods with nature. If we are really are connected to the homes we live in, then it is entirely possible that any changes in their construction and their contents may have an adverse effect on our health.

New construction methods

Over the last 60 years, there have been very big changes in the basics of house building, with the biggest shift taking place in the 1970s. In the early part of that decade most homes were fitted with central heating, which massively increased comfort levels. Then later in the decade came the oil crisis, and the cost of fuel rose sharply, making heat conservation a very important issue. A huge amount of resources were then diverted into making modern homes well insulated, and as a result they simply stopped breathing. Bau Biologists recognize that this method of construction is a major threat to our good health.

Now, we are discovering that there are health implications with the lifestyle to which we have become accustomed and, possibly, very attached. Many people are living in homes that have increasing levels of man-made radiations from computers, TVs, stereos, and other electrical equipment.

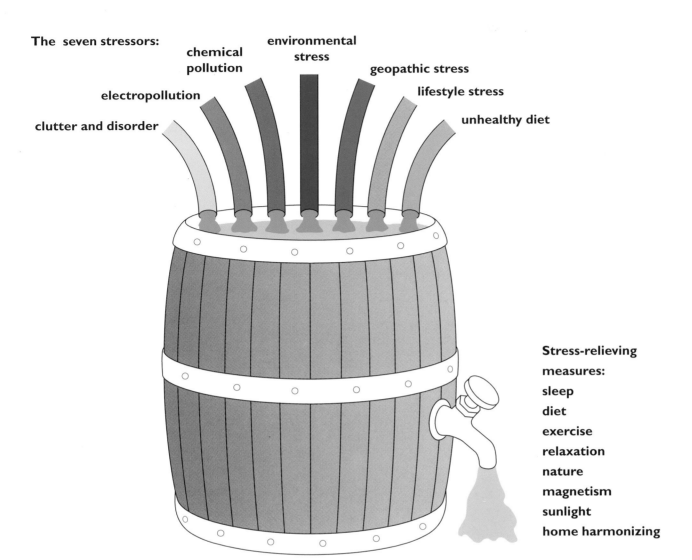

The seven stressors:

clutter and disorder

electropollution

chemical pollution

environmental stress

geopathic stress

lifestyle stress

unhealthy diet

Stress-relieving measures:
sleep
diet
exercise
relaxation
nature
magnetism
sunlight
home harmonizing

The water barrel

The concept of the water barrel is a simple way of explaining how different stresses in our home and life can affect us. Think of the water inside the barrel as the level of stress, which gradually fills up from the different pipes pouring into it. When the water level reaches the top and starts overflowing, that represents us becoming ill. The lower the level in the barrel, the healthier we are. What we have to do to keep in balance is to reduce the water coming in through the pipes. So here, as shown in this diagram, we need to focus on each of the inlet pipes representing clutter, electropollution, chemical pollution, environmental stress, geopathic stress, lifestyle stress, and an unhealthy diet, and work on each of them so that we reduce

their ability to fill the barrel. In addition to altering how the water flows into the barrel, or where our efforts are not effective enough, we need to turn on the spigot so that water can be released from the bottom of the barrel.

Ways of turning on the spigot to reduce the stresses effectively include sleep, good diet, exercise, getting in touch with nature, relaxation, magnetism, sunlight, and creating harmony in our homes. The aim is to incorporate all these de-stressing techniques into our daily lives. If we pay attention to our environment, wherever we are, we minimize the flow of each of the stressors mentioned above into our lives and can expect to live a healthier, happier life full of vitality and hope.

It is my view that depression has a direct correlation with the stress caused by these electromagnetic fields. Prozac is such a spectacularly successful drug, now reported to have been taken by 35 million globally, and I would make a connection between the use of this drug and the dominating presence of technology in our lives. In the light of this, depression has the potential to become a new world epidemic. It is currently the major cause of the loss of a productive life in 15–44 year olds and, together with other mental problems, represents 25 percent of all illness in Europe. In May 1999, 330 million people worldwide were estimated to be suffering from depression, and each year in America 19 million adults develop a depressive illness.

The modern lifestyle of luxury, excess, and technological reliance that we have created and adapted to is beginning to be more widely linked to health issues. My experience has shown that we are suffering from toxins that are contained in cleaning materials, furnishings, and fabrics. Even the very food we eat and the water we drink has been identified as being laden with high levels of pesticides and chemicals because these were thought to be the best way to provide us with pest-free fruit and vegetables and clean water.

Over this period of material prosperity it is true that in many ways the health of Western nations has deteriorated and I would link that to the way we live. Many people's lives are imbalanced by stress, and this will often result in both physical and mental suffering. In Britain, for example, the leading cause of death is cardiovascular disease, and this condition includes heart attacks, stroke and heart failure, and government statistics show that this accounts for 275,000 victims a year. This is followed by cancer, which claimed the lives of 157,000 in 1996 and, according to figures issued by the Cancer Research Campaign (CRC), accounts for 27 percent of all deaths in Europe (25 percent in the UK). The CRC claim that 70 percent of cancers have some connection with an unhealthy lifestyle, with 250,000 new cases diagnosed in the UK every year. Health experts now believe that stress is one of the main triggers of these conditions, currently the biggest killers in the Western world. So if we can find ways of managing our stress more effectively then we stand a better chance of avoiding ill health.

In addition to protecting ourselves from these diseases, it is also becoming clear that there are a growing number of conditions from which people suffer every day that erode wellbeing and diminish quality of life. Allergic ailments and conditions such as asthma and diabetes also seem to be on the increase. Asthma, strongly associated with environmental toxins and air quality, now has 3.4 million sufferers in the UK, with three times as many adults affected as 20 years ago. One in seven children (aged 2–15) now suffer symptoms. It is estimated that there are ten to twenty times more allergy sufferers in the UK than in the 1960s, with 50 percent of Americans suffering some kind of allergy. Fertility levels in many industrialized countries have dropped, and this is believed to be linked to chemicals in wate and, pesticides on food, as well as exposure to computer radiation. For men in the UK, this has dropped by an incredible 50 percent in the last 60 years.

The incidence of diabetes, a condition that is associated with the over-consumption of the sugary and processed foods that have become more and more popular over the last 40 years, is expected to treble to 3 million in the UK over the next decade while there are 123 million sufferers worldwide. The British Diabetic Association says that in addition to the 1.4 million sufferers in 2000 there are a further one million people suffering the condition who are as yet undiagnosed. And bearing in mind the increasingly sedentary lifestyles that we have, it is disturbing to hear of research from Harvard (published in 1999) in a study of 40,000 men over 10 years. They determined that those people who watched an average of 40 hours a week of TV were twice as likely to develop diabetes as those who watched less than two.

Many people are getting used to living more restricted lives, managing their pain and discomfort because they believe their symptoms are simply the signs of getting older. But good health is not just an absence of disease, it is about having vitality and feeling joyful. This can become a real possibility if we rethink our diet and include more organic food, and make changes to our environment that are recommended throughout this book. Look at your home with new eyes, and consider what changes you can make to bring your health and life back into balance.

ONE

The Seven Stressors

Our ability to cope with everyday events is a reliable indicator of our physical, mental, and emotional health. This chapter considers seven aspects of life and our environment that cause stress – clutter and disorder, electromagnetic radiation, chemical pollution, environmental stress, geopathic stress, lifestyle stress, and an unhealthy diet. Each has a major impact on our health and wellbeing. Although a single stressor may be handled individually without unbalancing the body too much, the cumulative effect of a few can be extremely harmful to our physical and mental wellbeing.

"Space and light and order. These are the things men need just as much as they need bread or a place to sleep."
Le Corbusier

Our home is another aspect of ourselves. It is our outer reality, reflecting what is happening inside us and in our lives. The way your home looks and is managed becomes a barometer for not only our physical health, but also our mental, emotional, and spiritual well-being. If your home is tidy and ordered it goes hand-in-hand with a well-structured and supportive routine. Similarly, if you live in a chaotic space, or one that is extremely cluttered, it represents a lifestyle that may be confused, lethargic, and lacking in energy. The more items you have tucked away, such as long-forgotten photo albums and bags of

RIGHT The need to collect objects can be a difficult habit to break. At a certain point the physical stuff starts to take over your space – and your life. Clutter, especially above your head, can represent your life crowding in on you. Clear your space and free up your life.

FAR RIGHT Having your clothes organized, especially your work clothes, will allow you to have a calm and orderly start to your day. Not having everything to hand when you are in a hurry can be stressful, and you may carry that stress around with you all day.

unwanted clothes, the more they reflect stagnation in your life and the need for you to cleanse out toxins hidden away deep inside.

An over-crowded environment will drain your vitality and make it difficult for positive energy to flow around your home. It can be depressing and blocks your connection to your spiritual and intuitive side. Having a good clear-out gives your creativity and inner wisdom a real boost.

Clutter in the home is very much a late 20th-century disease. Most people in the Western world suffer from having too many possessions, and at the same time have too little time to do the things they want to do. In short, our lives are much too full. Consider how your crowded life might match the saturation that exists in your home. Look at your cupboards and drawers and see how many of them are overflowing. Review the contents of your closet, and ask yourself

what percentage of your clothes are worn frequently, and how many you have not worn for a couple of years or longer. Research has shown that most of us only regularly wear about 20 percent of our clothes. Also consider whether your clothes still reflect who you are now, or have you moved on from the time when you first bought them?

The definition of clutter

Clutter is anything that makes you feel down, depressed, or sad when you look at it or think about it. It can be defined as anything that is:
- *Not regularly used.*
- *Not loved or cherished.*
- *Stored or left in the wrong place.*
- *Half-finished, such as knitting or a craft project.*
- *Squeezed into too small a space.*
- *Broken objects and appliances that cannot be used until they are fixed.*
- *An unwanted gift.*

Some people like to collect large collections of themed objects. Sometimes what starts out as an amusement with buying a couple of china frogs, for example, can very soon become a huge collection if all your friends use them as a theme for presents. Collections are fine if they really mean something and are appreciated, but they can get out of hand. So when you look at your shelves full of dolls, teapots, spoons or rabbits, you have to ask yourself if they really represent who you are now or who you want to become. If they don't, it is time to consider letting go of them.

Remember, everything in our environment is communicating with or affecting us on some level, and symbols always connect to our subconscious mind.

ABOVE Having plenty of good shelving supports our best intentions to be tidy. Review your shelves at least quarterly to see what you are storing. Move anything that is not useful or is out of date.

How clutter affects you

Having too many items in a room makes the room feel very restricted. Too much furniture, too many pictures on the wall, or too many ornaments on shelves means the background decoration can hardly be seen, and the space feels congested and tight. You will probably feel drawn to another, more relaxing room, where your eyes are not so distracted and the energy can move more freely.

If you have piles of unread magazines and newsletters, unopened mail, unfinished knitting projects, or objects waiting to be returned to their shelf after use, their negative effect will accumulate over time. They will begin to restrict you physically, and you will find yourself having to move around them. This restriction becomes a metaphor for some aspect of your life where you compromise and settle for less, and end up accepting not having life the way you really want. The clutter tends to restrict the energy of a room, making it slow and heavy, which will eventually create problems for you.

Why you need to clear clutter

In order for your life to run smoothly, you need to ensure that the energy flows easily through your home. It is when energy gets blocked that events and circumstances in your life get blocked, too. Remove the physical obstacles that exist in your space, and you will clear any impediments to your success.

Living in an environment that is cluttered and disordered confuses you and takes away your clarity and your decision-making skills, making it harder for you to decide how to progress and move forward. Your outer world reflects your inner life, so accumulating clutter is also very unhealthy as it slows down the energy flow in the interior, and consequently the life force within us. One of the most important areas to clear of unused objects is your home's entrance and hallway to allow the space to "breathe in" the necessary energy. The analogy is that if you impede this energy flow with clutter and unnecessary furniture, then you may also create respiratory problems for the occupants.

Clearing clutter is a most powerful way of taking control of your life. Sorting through and letting go of unwanted possessions and junk allows you to move on and makes a space for new opportunities to come into your life.

When you have made sure that your home is clear, and, so, symbolically your life, you will find that things have a tendency to fall within your preferred pattern. Unexpected checks can arrive, or you may hear from a long-lost friend. I have often found that when I am in need of something or someone, that they manage to appear on cue, out of nowhere, as if I have paved the way for them to show up.

The antidote to a complex life is to create simplicity

There is a movement that started in the US called Voluntary Simplicity, which reflects a search for more of a sense of balance in life. The philosophy is centered around the need to create a life that is outwardly simple but inwardly rich. This relates to the fact that the more you have, the less freedom you have because you then become responsible and it becomes attached to your psychic energy field. Voluntary Simplicity advocates a life of greater consciousness, where you become nourished more by your connection to spirit and nature and less by material goods and status. It is not about poverty or minimalism, it is about having awareness of the implications of everything you do or buy on others and the planet.

How to get rid of your clutter

• *Take one step at a time, start with one drawer, then progress to a whole cupboard, and you will find that you cannot hold back from tackling a whole room – it gets easier the more you do.*

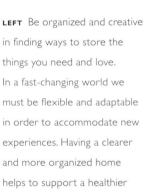

LEFT Be organized and creative in finding ways to store the things you need and love. In a fast-changing world we must be flexible and adaptable in order to accommodate new experiences. Having a clearer and more organized home helps to support a healthier state of mind.

ABOVE Dripping faucets should be repaired and dead batteries replaced. If you leave them, they will drain your energy.

ABOVE RIGHT Never leave anything that breaks, but fix it right away. Don't wait until it starts to annoy you. Keeping up with home maintenance is an investment, not only in your home but in yourself.

- *Motivate yourself by focusing on why you want more energy and more opportunities to come to you. It may seem unbelievable, but I have known people to have received checks (many sizeable ones) within days of removing full bags of trash. Try it for yourself.*
- *Try cleansing your home using home-harmonizing techniques (see pages 108–110). They will help you to shift energy if you are having trouble getting started.*
- *Get a friend to help you. Friends can be more ruthless and less emotional when you are reluctant to let something go.*
- *Clear the clutter from your attic, and get rid of those things that are hanging over you in life. Check down in the basement, if you have one, and find out what is stored there that is niggling your subconscious about unresolved past issues.*
- *Create a sense of order in your life by having everything at your fingertips just when you need it. Take the time to organize your work and study space since this will save time later and reduce possible stress.*

- *Introduce clutter clearing as a practice throughout your whole life, not just in your home – look at your diary, your commitments, rationalize your computer files, look at all the ways you use your time.*
- *Expect to see some energy or health adjustment as you rearrange things externally. In the same way that unpleasant clouds of dust can be created by a good clear-out, it can also happen in your body, so that you may feel worse before you feel better.*
- *Look at an object and ask yourself if you love it. If you do not, and it is not useful, then get rid of it.*
- *Give away unwanted gifts from relatives and friends. Don't feel guilty or let things clutter up your space just because they were precious to somebody else.*
- *When you buy a new item, clear out something else that is old.*
- *Be clear on who you are and what you want (see treasure map on page 70). When you move into a new role or phase of life, it helps to evaluate your possessions in terms of the future you and not the old you. It makes you recognize that many items of clothing and books were part of a phase that is no longer appropriate.*

Home maintenance

Maintaining all the electrical or mechanical items in your home is important. When you are living among things that don't work, it robs you of vital energy and is another source of stress. Get your house in order and make sure that everything works. Call the plumber to repair the leak, fix that cracked drainpipe, throw out the broken iron, or change that light bulb. Don't let these problems mount up and drain your energy any longer; don't even put them on a "to do" list – just act immediately to get them sorted out!

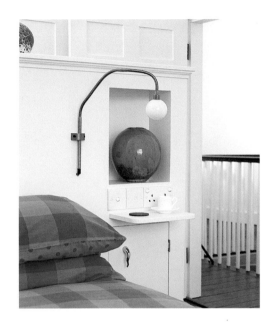

ABOVE There is just as much electropollution inside our homes as outside – and in some cases it can be worse. Our homes are totally wired to provide power everywhere at the touch of a button.

LEFT An increasing number of studies show that homes near electricity supply lines are more adversely affected than those farther away. Power cables, radio broadcasting, and cellular telecommunications transmitters are an increasing source of electropollution from outside our homes.

Long before electricity was discovered, the natural world was pervaded by rhythmically changing, life-supporting electromagnetic fields. These include the daily bathing of the earth's surface in sunlight with its warming far infrared waves and the continuing gentle oscillation of the earth's natural magnetic field. When we talk about electromagnetic fields (EMFs) being damaging, it is the emissions from human-made sources that are the issue, such as radio wave signals and microwaves. Some frequencies are believed by an increasing number of scientists and laypeople to be harmful, and the terms electro-smog and electropollution describe the unwelcome nature of some of the frequencies. The EMFs around our homes represent a growing health hazard, yet very little is known about them by the average householder. The EMFs we create have an unnatural resonance that makes more of an assault on our bodies.

Where do EMFs come from?

The television and radio broadcasting network generates a huge background electromagentic field around the world, and now, of course, there is the additional question of radiation from cellular telephones.

Apart from communications systems, the other source of radiation is the supply of electricity through overground cables carried by pylons. Radiation is also experienced when you travel in cars, trains, and planes. Thousands of international studies carried out are listed in the *Handbook of Biological Effects of Electromagnetic Fields* by C. Polk and E. Postow, looking at the effects of electropollution. Many of the results have highlighted concerns about the higher incidence of illness and cancer in those living in homes near to power supply lines, for example.

Inside the home, we can be affected by the wiring that runs throughout the structure of the building as well as our choice of different electrical appliances. Everything powered by electricity radiates an electromagnetic field from its wiring and also through the appliance. The location of these appliances, when and how often we use them, and the type and routing of the wiring have an impact on our health. Nearly all homes wired for electricity have some level of unwanted and harmful EM radiation. The radiation from electrical circuits continues even when we have unplugged all appliances and turned the lights off. What you need to find out is how much and decide what can be done to mitigate it.

How EMFs affect our bodies

EMFs affect everybody, but we each have different sensitivities to them. Alasdair Philips of Powerwatch, a consumer support and advice service in the UK on electromagnetic radiation issues, says that around 5 percent of the population are deemed to be highly sensitive to electrical fields, and tests on these people have shown that they experience real, physiological damage to their peripheral nerves. These people will feel uncomfortable in an electrically overloaded environment long before anyone else, but it doesn't mean that only they are being compromised.

Since the communication between cells is regulated by tiny electromagnetic signals, EMFs can cause problems in the body by, for example, suppressing the immune system's ability to protect us from invading bacteria and viruses. Exposure to high EMFs, particularly around the head, can interfere with the efficiency of the pineal gland, a part of the endocrine system that

What ailments are EMFs linked with?

My practical experience points to the fact that regular exposure to EM radiation has a definite association with various ailments such as depression, immuno-deficiency diseases, ME, Alzheimer's disease, childhood leukaemia, and cancer. Early symptoms of such diseases can be general fatigue, lack of concentration, mood swings, and reduced efficiency, also symptoms of exposure to EM radiation.

No single organization has proved conclusive links to high EM radiation and these diseases – and yet I feel strongly that this connection is something that we should not ignore and should take positive steps to reduce the impact of.

The soft tissue areas that project from the body – namely ears, breasts, and testicles – are particularly sensitive to microwave radiation and with the potential therefore to cause future health problems. This is an evolving area of research and it is estimated that it can take an average of 10–30 years before negative effects are detected in adult bodies.

The problem with EMFs today

Until the 1920s when radio broadcasting began, the only electromagnetic fields we experienced were the natural resonances of the earth. All life forms have evolved in this vibration but it has changed rapidly during the 20th and into the 21st century when radiation has increased from almost nothing in 1900 to levels millions of times higher 100 years later. First radio transmissions went out into the airwaves, then radar, which was followed by television and now microwave radiation for the cellular phone networks that surround us. This mixture of radiation is so "noisy" and obtrusive that it cuts us off from the earth's soothing, natural resonance.

ABOVE The average living room is full of modern electrical toys, including TVs and hi-fi systems. When we try to relax in these high EM fields, we can feel even more tired and sleepy just from the equipment.

RIGHT It is especially important to ensure that you do not have high EM fields near your head in your bedroom, as they will disturb the restoring quality of your sleep.

releases the hormones melatonin and serotonin. Melatonin controls the body's daily rhythms as well as our waking and sleeping patterns. Sleep problems are generally associated with a deficiency of melatonin. The same thing applies to lethargy, psychological disorders, immuno-deficiency, and mood changes. Placing your head in an EM field such as that generated by a hair dryer or an electric clock radio before bed can significantly reduce the level of this sleep-inducing hormone. Serotonin is believed to control our moods and states of consciousness, and, when it is depleted, it has been found to have strong links with depression.

LEFT The World Health Organization published research from Sweden in 1984 by Professors Johansson and Aaronsson that showed that after four hours' exposure in front of a computer screen the body's ability to cope with stress is severely affected and the time taken to recover is longer than the period of time many people spend away from their office – 15 hours. Over a period of a week, tiredness will build up, and many people will experience insomnia and abnormal exhaustion, an increasing tendency to make mistakes, and in many cases hormonal disturbances and loss of libido. A protection device will limit the effects of this radiation.

Our bodies need to be in harmony. They are designed to adapt to constant and gentle electromagnetic rhythms from the earth, but find it hard to cope with the intense radiation frequencies to which they are now being subjected. Safety boards in various countries have decreed industry safety levels for EMFs which relate more to acute exposure than to the low levels to which we are exposed daily.

I have seen evidence that constant exposure to EM radiation can put a body (or parts of it) into a vulnerable state making it more prone to serious illness. It can remain that way until a trigger comes along to activate cancer.

Recent research from Scandinavia supports the view that more and more people, particularly regular users of computers and cellular phones, are becoming electrically sensitive. These people then start to develop a range of symptoms when they come into contact with even the mildest of EM fields. They can also become much more sensitive to chemicals. Powerwatch estimates that an amazing 20 percent of the UK population in 2000 are electrically sensitive, a jump from 10 percent in 1990.

EM safety levels that have been set by Western authorities, including the International Commission on Non-ionizing Radiation Protection (most recently in 1998), only concentrate on exposure to high doses of radiation, which can cause overheating and electrocution, rather than the low doses to which we are constantly exposed. However, many scientific experts now feel that it is the long-term effects that are more dangerous, believing it is more harmful to be exposed to a small dose of EM radiation for a longer period of time than a larger dose for a short time.

Tips for reducing EMFs

- *Measure EM fields (see page 28–29) in all the rooms in your home, especially near to the sitting or sleeping areas.*
- *Try to move chairs and beds away from where high EMF levels are detected.*
- *Shield any new wiring in earthed metal conduits.*
- *Earth two-wire equipment such as laptop computers, desk lamps, and bedside lamps with metal bases or shades to lower the radiation.*
- *Walls that have high fields can be screened by lining with earthed metal foil.*
- *Consider installing circuit-breaking which automatically turn off the power supply at night, and only have electricity running through those circuits when it is needed for either turning on a light or an appliance.*

How to protect yourself from EMFs

- *People who feel that they are becoming electrically sensitive should avoid clothes made from synthetic materials since these amplify EMFs. Instead, wear natural materials such as cotton, wool and silk, especially for underwear.*
- *Eat unrefined and unprocessed foods in order to balance your own energy system.*
- *Build up your own energy by taking up exercise systems like tai chi, qi gong, aikido, and yoga.*
- *Wear products to increase your own energy field so that you are less debilitated by EM radiation. These include magnetic insoles (see page 104) and special personal protection devices.*
- *Avoid drying your hair at night with a hair dryer since it can affect sleep.*
- *Ideally, use a hair dryer with the electrical motor unit screwed to the wall and a separate nozzle for blowing hot air, which does not have electricity running through it (similar to those used in hotels).*

Using protective devices

I have seen the successful use of protection devices, such as special pendant necklaces that can protect the biological system of our bodies from harmful electromagnetic interference (see www.thehealthyhome.com). These devices are designed to correct the resonance of the body and realign it to its natural frequency. They do not always work with everybody, so investigate different ones and choose one that offers a money-back guarantee.

Using computers

A computer screen exposes you to a huge source of radiation and is more of a problem for those who work with computers throughout the day. Screens help to filter these rays but get less efficient as they age. Most manufacturers now produce monitors with special coatings to reduce significantly the electrical field of radiation. This makes most filter screens unnecessary, but there still remains a problem with light radiation and magnetic waves.

Experiments in France have also shown that sperm cells die when they are exposed to the radiation from a computer monitor with a cathode ray tube (this applies to most PCs except the new flatscreens and laptops). I believe that this is also connected to the fact that fertility in Western countries has dropped noticeably. Research featured in the October 1997 issue of *Psychology Today* shows that male fertility, in particular, has dropped by 50 percent in the last 60 years alone. In the 15 years from

LEFT This television is enclosed within a cupboard, so it can be closed when not in use. If you must have electrical equipment in your bedroom then make a point of unplugging everything before you go to sleep. Remember not to have your TV on standby overnight.

RIGHT Many homes now have a computer, so be especially careful with children using them. They will be sitting within two feet of the screen radiation, so it is important to restrict hours of usage and to install a protection device so that you can reduce the effect on their growing bodies.

FAR RIGHT Test findings from the British Defence Establishment Research Agency showed that signals from cellular phones can disrupt parts of the brain in charge of memory and learning. There is growing concern for the link between phone usage and brain tumors, and the fact that pregnant women and children are particularly at risk.

1971 to 1986, the incidence of testicular and prostate cancer has increased by 52 percent and 57 percent respectively.

Reading about the biological effects of pulsed electromagnetic radiations (PEMR) brings me to the conclusion that occupations that expose people to high EM fields, such as computer operators, record much higher rates of chronic fatigue, eye problems, and flu- and cold-type symptoms than other occupations. Regular exposure has been linked with a tendency to reduce sex drive, concentration, and fertility and to increase the risk of a miscarriage. One UK study by Reading University at Southampton Health Authority found that neutralizing these radiations could reduce respiratory symptoms by 40 percent. The UK has roughly 50 million computers in use in the year 2000.

Tips for reducing computer stress

- *Use a protective device, preferably one that has been scientifically tested such as the Bioshield, to eradicate radiation effects from cathode ray screens of televisions and computers.*
- *Some people report that certain earth crystals such as natural quartz, fluorite, and black tourmaline can be placed next to a computer to soak up some of the EM emissions.*
- *If you work regularly at a computer, then ensure that you take regular breaks as you work throughout the day. Get advice about about any barrier devices that can be used to reduce the effects of the radiation. If you have regular headaches and eye strain then talk to your employer and discuss ways of avoiding continual exposure to EM emissions from computers.*

EMFs and television screens

The monitors of television and video games have cathode ray tubes, which produce noxious radiation when light is projected through them. This is particularly detrimental to children, whose growing bodies are more susceptible.

Professor Marcel Rufo of the University of Marseilles published a study on 289 young children in 1990, that was carried out over six months. This has shown that there is a likelihood that if young children spend more than 50 minutes a day in front of a TV or computer screen, this could be a contributing factor to a decline in their performance at school, their memory being affected, and their becoming more aggressive.

Experiments published by Jacques Surbeck of Anox Technology show that just 20 minutes in front of a TV is enough to soak a child's brain with electromagnetic radiation, making it harder for the two sides of their brain (left and right) to communicate. Understanding and, therefore, learning is dependent on this function, and this adverse effect can last up to four hours after exposure to a TV screen.

The detrimental effects of the radiation start to diminish at a distance of about 8–12 ft (2.4–3.6m) from the TV screen but, unfortunately, most children prefer to sit very close, especially when they are using a games monitor. A safe distance is equivalent to eight times the diagonal of the screen.

The EMFs produced by electrical equipment are not only invisible, but the magnetic element produces waves that are extremely harmful as they are not stopped by filters, walls, lead aprons, or the human body. The imperceptible flickering of the TV screen creates oscillations that cause abnormal responses in the brain, bringing about headaches, eye strain, and fatigue. They also interfere with our immune system's ability to produce the cells (T-Lymphocytes) that fight infections.

Tips for reducing television stress

- *Sit farther away from the television set.*
- *Install a protective device (for the latest products see www.thehealthyhome.com).*
- *Reduce the number of hours that you watch TV.*
- *Monitor how often children watch TV.*

Using cellular phones

It is estimated that nearly 40 percent of people in Europe and 50 percent in the UK have a cellular phone, and this is likely to double by 2005. There has been a lot of press coverage over the safety of cellular phones. Loss of memory, headaches, and premature aging are some of the key issues, but of greatest concern is the possibility that brain tumor growth may be stimulated by the radiation being placed directly against a user's head. The radiation goes straight through the skull into the brain. A hands-free facility where the user wears an earpiece reduces this risk by about 80 percent, but wearing them (and personal beepers) anywhere on the body can be problematic because the current is channeled down the energy lines of the body, creating problems elsewhere.

Tips for reducing cellular phone stress

- *Protect your head by buying a radiation shield for your cellular phone, or buy a hands-free attachment.*
- *Install an aerial to use your cellular phone in the car in conjunction with a hands-free attachment, because emissions while moving can be 50 times greater as the phone searches for a signal.*
- *Try to reduce metal objects worn on the body – such as belts with big buckles, metal-framed eyeglasses, and underwired bras – since they can pick up radiation from your cellular phone and amplify it fivefold around your body.*
- *Restrict the use of your phone to essential calls only to reduce your exposure to radiation.*
- *Protect your energy by fielding it with magnetic insoles.*

Testing radiation from a TV or computer screen

Get someone to stand in front of a TV (preferably in the place where they would normally sit) that is turned off, and test their muscle strength by asking them to stretch out their arm at shoulder height. Place one hand on their shoulder and the other on their lower arm or hand with palm facing down. Press down, asking them to use their strength to resist the pressure. The degree to which they are able to hold up their arm gives you a baseline measurement to work from.

Now get them to stand in front of a TV that is turned on, again in the place where they would normally sit, with their stomach facing it. Repeat the exercise using exactly the same pressure. You should see that there is less resistance – less muscle strength – with the TV turned on. You can repeat the exercise a third time, with the protection device on the TV and notice the difference. With protection there is likely to be no reduction in resistance, so that strength is maintained. You can also try the same test with a person wearing magnetic insoles.

This experiment can also be tried in front of a computer. Further guidance on these tests is available on www.thehealthyhome.com.

Dowsing to establish EMF levels

Dowsing is an alternative way of establishing the radiation from a television or computer (see dowsing for geopathic stress page 65). The rods will determine how far radiation extends from the television when they cross each other.

When the exercise is repeated with a protection device on the television, you will notice that the extent of the radiation will be considerably less.

Installing new wiring for EMF protection

The following instructions for installing new wiring should be carried out only by a qualified electrician.

1 *Get the electrician to use sheathed wire or wire encased in a metal conduit.*

2 *Install a circuit breaker so that electrical current is not flowing around the home when not required. Electrical power will come back into the circuit on demand.*

3 *Ask the electrician to create a ring circuit with a loop back so that the magnetic field will not be high if there is a wiring problem. The wire needs to go right round the circuit and double back on itself instead of coming into the ring one way and leaving at the end of the single loop.*

Testing existing wiring and appliances

1 *Buy or rent a hand-held testing device to measure both the electric and magnetic fields in the home (see www.thehealthyhome.com).*

2 *Go around the house one room at a time. Hold the device both against and near each piece of electrical equipment in each room.*

First measure the magnetic field, then take the electrical reading. The levels to aim for are:
- *0.04 Microtesla for a magnetic field*
- *Less than 10 volts per metre (vpm) for an electric field.*

3 *Take a reading with the meter sitting on the equipment (such as a computer), and then move the device away to see just how far the field extends.*

4 *The most important reading to note is the one that covers the area where you are sitting or sleeping in relation to the equipment. For example, if you sit at a computer, take the reading out to your chest area. If you are measuring a wall heater, take a reading at the nearest place someone would be likely to sit next to it.*

5 *After you have measured the fields of all equipment in a room, measure the walls, floor and surfaces. You are looking for "hot spots"; these are high concentrations of energy fields coming from either equipment or wiring. For example, you may find a section of wall with a high reading that you can not find a source for. It could be the wiring inside the walls and you can check this by turning off various circuits at the main electrical supply. Alternatively, investigate the other side of the wall, where you may find the source is the electricity meter or an electrical oven in your kitchen or your neighbor's apartment.*

6 *Check your desk computer, testing where the emissions are strongest by holding a radio tuned to a medium-wave (AM) radio station. Note the area where the interference occurs.*

7 *High electrical readings can be remedied with earthing and circuit breakers, but high magnetic readings are more of a problem and will require professional help.*

CHEMICAL POLLUTION

In recent years people have become increasingly aware of the threat of environmental pollution on a global scale, much of which is caused by chemicals. There are far fewer who are aware of the pollution that also exists within our homes. These odorless and colorless poisons have become a part of our lives for the last 30–40 years and are released from cleaning products, but more insidiously from synthetic materials used in the home and the pesticides that exist in many foods. Allergies and other illnesses are becoming everyday problems as this exposure takes its toll on our bodies.

The worthy campaigns to save home energy costs have backfired on themselves and stopped our houses from being able to breathe out all the toxins that we are bringing in.

While the popularity of health and organic foods has been on the increase for some time, the interest in ecologically-friendly products has been less sustained. And even when people buy these, they often do not take the same care with buying paints, home-improvement products, or furnishings, which often contain the chemicals they have previously rejected.

Slowly this attitude is beginning to change, helped by European countries such as Germany which has been at the forefront of introducing the concept of "eco" labeling and integrating healthy-living products into the home. Interest is also now also growing in the rest of Europe, the United States and Australia.

The growing problem

In the last few decades there has been a huge increase in the number of petrochemicals used for packaging and making furniture and fabrics. Of the chemicals manufactured every year little is known about their long-term effects.

Most homes and offices are now filled with synthetic substances that are believed to be responsible for headaches and mild depression, niggling, annoying conditions that are not life-threatening but which bring us down and help to erode our sense of wellbeing.

Environmental pollution is now a factor being investigated as significant in affecting a variety of conditions such as asthma, emphysema, nervous disorders and depression, Alzheimer's and Parkinson's disease, as well as different types of cancer. A study at Stanford University Medical School, for example, reported in May 2000 that research points to the fact that people who use insecticides in their homes are twice as likely to develop Parkinson's disease.

In 1980, the American Toxic Substances Strategy Committee issued a report indicating that 80–90 percent of cancers are triggered by some exposure to hazardous substances in the environment. Acute exposure to chemical substances can cause an immediate reaction, but this will often not do any long-lasting damage. However, chronic exposure over a longer period of time can be much more deadly simply because we are not aware of it and the negative effects, which are accumulative, may not appear for decades.

Few of the chemicals used legally in everyday household items have been tested for levels of toxicity. In her book *Home Safe Home*, Debra Lynn Dodd points out that next to nothing is known about the toxic effects to humans of almost 80 percent of the more than 48,000 chemicals listed by the Environmental Protection Agency (EPA). A national Research Council Study found that complete health hazard evaluations were available for only 10 percent of pesticides. There is growing concern that the

symptoms that result from long-term, low-level exposure can be wrongly attributed to normal aging. The subtle symptoms can be fatigue, headaches, inattentiveness, general malaise, and dermatitis. With the exception of skin ailments and breathing problems, it can be virtually impossible to connect the other conditions to a chemically-laden environment.

Toxicity affects everyone differently, but it is only logical to assume that it will have the most impact on more vulnerable people such as children, pregnant women, people over 60 years old, and those who spend more than 12 hours a day inside the home. Smokers and regular drinkers of alcohol, those who do not exercise regularly, and people who eat an inadequate diet are also more at risk.

Building solutions

Bau Biologie has previously been mentioned as a movement which grew out of Germany's massive rebuilding program in the aftermath of World War II. It combines a scientific approach to construction with a more holistic view of how people relate to buildings. Many people living in homes that were newly constructed using modern synthetic materials suffered from depression, insomnia, allergies, circulatory problems, and cancer. At this time a definite link between illness and the buildings people lived in was made.

Bau Biologie is about having an ecological awareness and an understanding of the impact of buildings on human health. Its goal is to bring humanity into harmony with the natural environment and technology. The human skin, clothing, and buildings are seen as one living system with different layers. The home is thought of as the third skin.

Some of Bau Biologie's basic concepts are to:

- *Use untreated, natural building materials.*
- *Incorporate wall, ceiling, and floor materials that will breathe naturally.*
- *Use organic paints and treatments.*
- *Locate dwellings some distance from factories, industrial buildings, and main traffic routes.*
- *Allow natural regulation of indoor humidity.*
- *Construct buildings with pleasant or neutral smells but no toxic fumes.*
- *Choose natural lighting bulbs and colors that relate to nature.*
- *Preserve natural electrical field conditions by not subjecting the occupants to inappropriate electromagnetic fields.*

The home toxins

The three major toxins that can be circulating inside the home for most of the time are VOCs (volatile organic compounds), combustion gases, and pesticides. These come from construction materials, paints, furnishings, and appliances. In addition to these, there are many other chemicals that are released when cleaning materials and other household products are used. These include pesticides, aerosol sprays, household paints, household cleaners, air fresheners, and cleaning fluids.

Because this toxicity comes from so many sources, the whole body system is affected and the symptoms that people experience become harder to diagnose.

Small doses of individual chemicals are generally accepted as causing little harm to people. However, long-term exposure is serious, and nobody really knows what we are creating when all the different substances are mixed together. Chemicals can even react together to increase toxicity. I have found evidence to show that the levels of toxins once considered safe are now no longer felt to be so.

Reactions to chemical toxicity can differ: some people can be very sensitive and have an acute reaction when exposed to high levels, suffering from immediate breathing problems, rashes, and headaches. The most dangerous are chronic delayed reactions resulting from daily exposure building up over time (this is where neurological damage and cancer are more likely to result). For example, lead in gasoline has been linked by some researchers with learning difficulties in children.

Allergy and asthma sufferers may be the first to notice irritating symptoms caused by chemical pollutants. People who are really sensitive to chemicals will have immediate problems with: car exhaust fumes, new carpeting, perfumes, detergents, and fabric softeners. One theory is that the chemicals that irritate hypersensitive people are actually poisonous to everyone. Their immediate reaction simply alerts the rest of us to the potential, silent dangers in the same way that a canary in a mineshaft would alert miners to potential hazards.

About 250,000 new chemical substances are created each year, with no single organization checking how harmful they are. Linda Mason Hunter's 1989 book *The Healthy Home* states that "4.5 million chemicals are known, 45,000 are in distribution. It takes a team of scientists, 300 mice, 2–3 years, $300,000 to determine whether a single suspect chemical causes cancer." Of the thousands of synthetic chemicals that are listed by the EPA in America, less than 10 percent have been tested for their chronic or mutagenic effects. Sensitivity to EMFs also seems to be increased by exposure to chemicals.

- *Some plasterboards are still made with phosphogypsum from power stations and give off radioactive emissions.*
- *Cavity wall insulation also cuts down on the building's ability to breathe. Some foams can outgas small levels of formaldehyde.*
- *Double-glazing has a metal frame or film that can conduct radiation.*
- *Structural timber is often treated with insecticide or high-grade poisons.*
- *Many floors are made of particle board, which emits formaldehyde and other chemicals.*

All of these materials are released slowly over many years. In short, modern buildings do not allow the natural radiations that are life-enhancing to come through; they further distort energies that are already negative; and they leak out dangerous chemicals from materials that are designed to keep us warm and keep out pests.

The increasing pollution

A study in the 1990s, *Spengler's Indoor Air Quality*, has shown that pollution inside the average home is 10 times greater than outside, even in areas that suffer from industrial smog.

The biggest change in our homes came when fuel-saving became so important in the 1970s and our homes were well insulated to prevent drafts and ensure lower energy consumption. In Britain, government grants were readily offered for people to do this. Buildings began to have a much slower movement of air, and often could not easily release the chemicals present in the atmosphere.

Over the last three decades a huge number of chemicals from construction, furniture, and paints have been introduced into the home. The air that we now breathe is likely to contain many chemicals. At room temperatures, products containing VOCs can release them into the environment. Furthermore, the addition to most homes of central heating means that warmer temperatures indoors encourages even more of the chemicals to be released.

Modern homes are two and a half times more energy efficient than older ones, and the familiar smell of a brand-new home is a mixture of the chemicals that come from the building materials. Construction has changed over the years, and 5,000 chemicals are now used in the materials used for house building. These are some of the main items used in modern building that are causing problems:

- *Today's concrete floors do not breathe, and make geopathic stress (GS) worse by dispersing it. Timber floors used in old properties allow ventilation and naturally deflect any GS.*

VOCs

This is the biggest group of pollutants, and two of the most toxic are formaldehyde and benzene. Formaldehyde, a noxious gas released from many furnishing materials and from glues in MDF (medium density fiberboard) and other grades of particle board, has been used in the construction and manufacturing industries for a century but it is only in the last few years that studies have begun to investigate possible links with cancer. Substitutes for formaldehyde, such as isocyanates, are more environmentally friendly but are believed to be just as harmful to our health.

Any homes that were built after 1980 contain three times the former levels of formaldehyde. More than 800 different VOCs have been detected in the air inside homes, given off by different building and furnishing materials.

LEFT People are increasingly choosing natural wood floors because they are easiest to keep clean and do not harbor dust and dust mites in the way carpets do. If you have rugs, then shake them regularly. If you have carpets, then vacuum the dust out of them every couple of days.

RIGHT Rush matting and other natural fiber floorcoverings are neutral, so do not create electro-static energy which encourages dust. They do not require any toxic adhesive and also help absorb sound on a wooden floor.

FAR RIGHT Research from the Salvatore Maugori Foundation in Italy found that houses in northern European cities had twice as much benzene as in the south. The chemical found in furnishings and gasoline fumes is thought to be absorbed by the furnishings favored in the homes in the colder climates rather than the tiled rooms of the south.

Although a high level of the gas is generally released when the material is newly installed, it also continues to emit odorless toxic fumes for up to a decade later.

Formaldehyde is believed to cause skin rashes, dizziness, breathing difficulties, nausea, and respiratory and allergy problems. Products that contain formaldehyde can be found in virtually every room of the average Western home, and include: upholstery, carpeting, wallpaper, adhesives, beauty products, permanent-press fabrics (including bed linens and curtaining). But the biggest source is the favorite material of DIY enthusiasts – MDF and other plywoods and boards that are made from pressing wood particles together. Pressed woods are used for sub-flooring, countertops, kitchen cabinets, paneling and furniture.

How to counteract VOCs

Placing several healthy plants around the home can help to clear and purify the air (see page 98 for which varieties are most effective). Try to be more aware of materials that contain the more toxic chemicals and restrict their usage. When you are considering using builders or making some home improvements yourself, choose real wood rather than pressed-particle board. The main issue with these boards involves the inhalation of dust during construction. Cutting and sanding represents a very chronic and serious risk of airborne formaldehyde.

PVC

Polyvinyl chloride is a versatile material used to make credit cards, packaging, and food-wrapping materials. It is a component of home furniture, toys and office equipment, plumbing materials, ductwork, and windows. Many of the raw materials involved in its manufacture are known toxins and carcinogens.

Limiting exposure to PVC

Choose non-PVC film for food protection, or cover with a natural material like cloth. Evaluate each purchase that you make, analyzing whether you really need it, and whether you can buy it in a natural material. Instead of PVC plumbing pipes, use polyethylene, a stable synthetic substance used in the body. Test your water for acidity before using copper pipes, as this encourages copper to leach from the pipes.

RIGHT A study by Bristol University found that women who cooked with gas had a one-third higher likelihood of developing a respiratory illness. By-products of gas central heating and cooking can affect breathing and be particularly problematic for those already prone to asthma and allergies. Keep your kitchen well-ventilated: open a window or door to bring in fresh air after cooking.

FAR RIGHT Approximately 20 percent of airborne dust comes from carpet fibre and 80 percent from skin cells. These particles soak up chemicals and are carbonized by TVs, making them a big irritant for those with respiratory problems. A wooden floor such as the one shown here will create far less dust in your home.

Pesticides

The EPA has determined that 80–90 percent of the pesticides that humans are exposed to occur inside the home. They are air borne, walked in on our shoes, and within our water supply. They impregnate fresh and processed foods, are added to carpeting, and are introduced through mothballs, flea collars, and aerosols. Even if you practice organic gardening you can still suffer exposure from the pesticides in neighbors' gardens. You can also be more at risk if you live near a public park or golf course that is known to use high levels of pesticides.

Limiting exposure to pesticides

Use a water filter for all cooking and drinking water, and ensure it reduces the effects of pesticides. Buy organic foods, which have been grown naturally, whenever you can. Be aware of what you bring in on your shoes, and take shoes off once inside the home, inviting any visitors to do the same. Apart from lowering the amount of pesticides walked all over your carpet, the carpets will need less cleaning. When buying carpets, choose natural ones made from wool that has not been treated with pesticides.

Use natural alternatives to pest control, choose low-toxic products, or even make your own. Let sunlight regularly flood into your home since it helps to break down pesticides, and make sure that your home is well ventilated.

Combustible gases

Gas stoves, ovens, and heating appliances, including central heating, give off toxic gases and particles that can prove harmful if they are not well managed. Carbon dioxide, carbon monoxide, nitrogen dioxide, and hydrocarbons are all released on a daily basis. In order to combat the bad effects, make sure appliances are regularly serviced and well ventilated.

If any of these fumes are allowed to build up in your home you and your family may as a result experience respiratory problems, headaches, dizziness, nausea, fatigue, and depression. Furthermore, we already know that faulty gas fires can be fatal. Carbon monoxide is a deadly gas: it is odorless, and small amounts can kill within hours. However, a slow seeping of small amounts over a long period will initially produce flu-like symptoms and loss of memory, therefore impairing people's ability to function properly.

Nitrogen dioxide is given off by gas stoves and ovens at very high levels. Preparing Sunday lunch where the stove or oven is used continuously with no ventilation creates a great deal of toxicity. I have heard a theory that women can suffer depression through the daily use of a gas stove.

Cigarette smoke is a pollutant within our homes. At least 40 of its 200 chemicals are known to be carcinogenic. Smoking can also reduce the level of negative ions, causing lethargy, discomfort, and lack of concentration.

Limiting exposure to gases

Get an expert to test for any gas leaks, and to check that all your appliances work properly with good ventilation. Also, make sure the extractor fan above your gas stove works effectively, and always open a window while cooking to completely air the kitchen.

Encourage any family members who smoke to give up, and declare your home a no-smoking zone. If you designate areas where you allow

smoking, ventilate them well by opening windows and adding groups of healthy green plants to help neutralize the effects of the chemicals that are left. Never allow smoking in a room used by children, who are much more sensitive and vulnerable to its adverse effects.

Radon gas

Radon is an odorless by-product of decaying uranium in the earth and is found in some parts of the country, depending on the bedrock. This radioactive gas rises through the subsoil,

seeping into the house as a gas and can accumulate in the basement. Radon is a carcinogen that does not cause any noticeable short-term effects, but exposure over many years in a home that has high levels can increase the chance of lung cancer. Smokers are twice as likely to be adversely affected by radon.

Minimizing the effects of radon

Discover if radon has been identified in the area where you live. If it is prevalent, get a specialist to check the levels and then to determine what

LEFT Many polycotton blend
materials have a formaldehyde
finish. Choose natural cotton
covers when you can.

ABOVE LEFT AND RIGHT Natural
linoleum is a good choice for
a floor because it is attractive,
durable, and completely
natural. Children and babies
can be 20 times more
susceptible to chemicals than
adults. As they are nearer the
floor, it is safer for them to
crawl around on a wood,
tiled, or lino floor rather than
a new, chemically treated
wool carpet or one made
of synthetic fibers.

kind of venting can be installed. Have a building specialist check your home structure for cracks and seal them. Radon is strongest at its source, so avoid using the basement as a living area in a house that is affected.

Flooring

Carpets and other types of floorcoverings used to be made of natural materials obtained from animals and plants. *The Natural House Catalog* by David Pearson states that two-thirds of the carpet yarn sold in the US are nylon and just a half of one percent are made from wool. The fumes from carpet glue have also been blamed for respiratory problems, nausea, fatigue, and memory loss. Formaldehyde and phenol both outgas (leach out) from synthetic carpets.

The use of synthetic materials also increases the level of positively charged ions in an interior, therefore producing high static electricity. This,

in turn, affects the serotonin content of the blood of those who spend time there, which can be linked to headaches and lethargic behavior.

Carpeted floors also tend to harbor more microorganisms than any other type of flooring. New carpet, especially when it comes direct from the factory, releases as many as 25–30 chemicals into the atmosphere, many of them chlorinated hydrocarbons that are used as pesticide to control fungi, mold, insects, and rodents. This mixture can be released for about three months. Jute backing, which is a natural fiber, is less harmful than rubber.

Healthy flooring alternatives

Rugs are a healthier option than carpets, particularly if they are made naturally and non-chemical dyes have been used.

Natural wood flooring can be a good alternative, but choose woods that come from sustainable sources, and check if they have had any chemical treatments. If you really want to use carpeting, buy ones with a high wool content and jute backing or which have natural fibers such as coir or rush matting.

Paints, varnish, and stains

In the US, where over a billion gallons of paint are sold each year, a study at John Hopkins University revealed that paint contained 300 toxic chemicals, of which 150 are known to be carcinogenic. There are four basic ingredients to chemical paints — resins for adhesion and hardness of the coating, solvents to keep the paint liquid and which evaporate after use, pigments for color, and additives to enhance the other components. They also contain fungicides and chemical preservatives. Paints are either gloss or eggshell finishes with oil-based solvents, or

headaches, chronic fatigue, eye and respiratory problems, irritability, mood swings, dizziness and nausea, impaired judgement and coordination, and joint and muscle pain. The toxic ingredients of paints and varnishes include formaldehyde, toluene, xylene, kerosene, ammonia, plastics, and ethanol. Many manufacturers now provide low-odor paints, and are phasing out the use of solvents, but many of the ingredients are still toxic, and are more harmful to the environment.

If you decide not to use organic paints (see below), wear an activated charcoal mask when decorating, and keep the rooms well ventilated. If you can, try not to use the room for several days after painting to let it settle down.

Healthy alternatives for paints

Natural and organic paints and finishes which do not use petrochemicals are now available. Ground-breaking manufacturers such as Auro in Germany produce completely natural paints with ingredients sourced from plants. Old-fashioned and original techniques are being revived to make paints such as casein, made from milk protein, and others from chalk, lime, and clay. Natural thinners for oil-based paints derived from citrus oils are now also available.

Wallcoverings

Wallpaper helps to prevent a small amount of heat loss and cover uneven wall surfaces. Many are made of vinyl or have a plastic finish on paper which stops the wall from breathing. Vinyl papers will emit vapors in a warm room, affecting people who are sensitive to chemicals. The adhesives used to paste the wallpaper onto the wall are normally non-toxic cellulose, but contain a fungicide. Heavy-duty papers need an adhesive that contains polyvinyl.

ABOVE A WHO report in 1989 claimed that paint can be a carcinogenic substance for those who use it. Avoid any bad effects by using natural, non-toxic paints.

RIGHT The through-colored clay plaster shown here needs no paint. It also compensates for changes in humidity, creating a very pleasant and stable environment.

water-based latex paints. The oil-based solvents are much more harmful because they release dangerous VOCs known to be factors in causing cancer and damage to the nervous system. In California, 50 percent of annual VOC emissions are estimated to come from paint, and that also includes oil refineries and fuel stations.

A British study by Anna Kruger in *H is for Ecohome* revealed that 93 percent of professional painters showed symptoms of solvent poisoning. Paints present problems, not only during their application and removal, but also throughout their life. Adverse effects include

Healthy alternatives for wallcoverings

Choose fabric papers and ones with waterproof finishes that let your walls breathe. Hand-painted, hand-printed papers, or natural fabrics including cotton and silk, are all suitable. There are now organic versions of paste available.

Think about painting plain plastered walls with organic paint, using paint effects to heighten the slightly rough effect. Wood paneling and burlap-type papers are also very attractive.

Furniture

Window blinds made from polyester fabrics and vinyl can be a problem, since when the sun shines through a window these materials will emit more gases, such as halogenated hydrocarbons and plasticizers, as they are heated.

Many modern sofas and chairs contain polyurethane foam, and this can cause bronchitis, coughs, and various skin problems. To cut costs, a lot of furniture is now made from MDF or particle board, and this unfortunately emits formaldehyde fumes.

Healthy alternatives for furniture

Use blinds that are made from natural cotton. Ideally, choose sofas and chairs that have cushions filled with natural fibers such as feathers and down. Also, when buying dining furniture, have a look at solid wooden styles with natural finishes made from sustainable sources. Choosing older or antique pieces of furniture means that they are likely to have already outgassed, or released, any harmful vapors.

Chemical pollutants in water

Water is essential for our survival – we could not exist for many days without it. More than 70 percent of our body weight is water, which constantly needs to be refreshed with pure water. It is important not just for drinking, but also bathing, cooking, and cleaning. Most people in developed countries assume that their water supply is safe because it smells fresh and looks clear, but for many householders it can hold an alarming quantity of pollutants.

Water is a strong solvent and it readily absorbs many nutrients, such as selenium, iodine, copper, and iron, which we find beneficial in small quantities. However, it will also take on many harmful substances. In the US, some 350 chemicals have been identified in drinking water including: herbicides, pesticides and nitrates from the soil, hazardous contaminants from landfill sites, chemical effluents and toxic wastes polluting rivers. When water is tested, many of these substances are found to be at higher levels than is legally safe. In the UK, toxic solvents from factory effluent have been linked to colon and stomach cancer.

In 1988 in southwest England, 20,000 tons of aluminum sulfate was accidentally added to drinking water. Many people reported a number of different symptoms, including eczema and memory loss. "Polluted" water will have a particularly strong effect on those suffering from allergies, chemical sensitivities, and skin disorders. For everybody else, health problems start from the slow build-up of small traces of the various toxins in the body.

Fluoridated water

The dental profession have long presented a strong case to convince the public that fluoridated water has a beneficial effect on teeth and bones, but little has really been known about how it affects the rest of the body. Many studies have shown that it affects body organs and the brain and nervous system. It may be partly

LEFT AND ABOVE There is a lot of advertising hype about the importance of washing kitchen surfaces with chemically-laden, anti-bacterial cleaners. However, these can wipe out the good microbes in our bodies and destroy our natural defense system. The safest way is old-fashioned scrubbing with hot water and a clean cloth or brush. Add teatree oil as a natural disinfectant or lemon to bleach stains.

responsible for hyperactivity and many puzzling illnesses such as Myalgic encephalomyelitis (ME or chronic fatigue syndrome). According to a report in the health bulletin *What Doctors Don't Tell You* in March 1999, there are similarities between chronic fatigue syndrome and the early stages of fluoride poisoning.

In Japan, a direct link between damage to the heart and dental fluorosis was found. The German Association of Gas and Water Employees prepared a detailed report concluding that fluoridation is foreign to nature, generally unnecessary, irresponsible, and harmful to the environment.

Unfortunately, you will be exposed to these toxins even in the shower. The toxic gas chloroform is released as steam from a hot shower with chlorinated water. A 10-minute shower exposes a person to 50 percent more volatile chemicals than by drinking half a gallon of the same water a day.

Ensuring a supply of healthy water

Boiling all water does not eliminate these toxins, so the solution is to filter all the water used in the home. There are several kinds of filter available, and your choice depends on the analysis of your water to find out what it contains. Most municipal water is from two sources. The first is surface supply (from rivers and reservoirs), which is vulnerable to agricultural pollution, industrial chemicals, and seepage from septic tanks. The second is underground wells, which can be contaminated by herbicides, radon, fertilizers, and pesticides.

The main domestic filtration systems are carbon filters, which remove chlorine and pesticides; reverse osmosis filters for bacteria and dissolved solids; and UV light filters, which kill microorganisms. Depending on the water you have, you can buy a different combination of filters. To find out what you need, have your water tested locally by your supply company to determine the best type of purification system.

Installing a filter or purification system for your drinking water is better than drinking bottled spring water. When traveling, drink from glass bottles since chemicals can leach from plastic ones into the water at higher temperatures. A water purification system will also reduce exposure to VOC gases in showers. It is also a good idea to change to a brand of fluoride-free toothpaste.

Chemical cleansers

High levels of organic compounds are found in aerosols, cleansers, and polishes. Research has found that they are linked to cancer and respiratory ailments as well as nausea and dizziness. Disinfectant, bleach, detergent, air freshener, oven cleaner, carpet shampoo, and toilet cleansers all contain a cocktail of chemicals that can prove harmful to us.

Aerosol sprays, which are fortunately now being used less and less, contain methylene, which is a carcinogen. Research at Bristol University (1999) among 14,000 women in the UK showed that those who were regular users of aerosol cleaning products often suffered headaches, and that 60 percent of all women reported experiencing regular headaches.

Pets can be particularly at risk from chemical residues: owners often clean their homes with a mixture of products and then go out leaving all the windows closed. Since pets are closer to floor level, they are much more susceptible to chemical fumes from a freshly disinfected floor, for example. Cats, especially, tend to lick their paws clean and may well pick up chemicals on them. As a result, many of the negative symptoms that people suffer from chemical toxicity will show up in their pets first.

Detergents

Modern laundry detergent ingredients include petrochemical surfactants for separating and removing dirt, phosphates to soften water and increase the power of the surfactants, and enzymes to break down protein stains.

Many of these ingredients not only damage human health, increasing the risk of eczema and allergies, but also have a great impact on wildlife in rivers and lakes. The substances are not biodegradable, and some of the chemicals are adversely affecting the fertility levels of fish. This water will ultimately be a source of drinking water, and could therefore be affecting human fertility levels.

Healthy alternatives to detergents

Most modern laundry detergents were designed to clean synthetic fabrics on which stains can be more stubborn. Indeed, the sale of more ecologically-friendly washing powders and cleaning agents would have grown more swiftly had fewer people not held onto the belief that real cleanliness comes from aggressive products. Consequently, products with more natural ingredients which can often do the job just as well are not considered to be as efficient.

Natural washing products

- *Borax, baking soda, washing soda, and natural soap can be used effectively. Grate soap and mix with water in a blender.*
- *Buy ecologically-friendly products from your local health food store.*

- Herbal vinegar will dissolve grease in washing water. Washing soda or borax are good dishwashing liquids in hard water areas.
- Lemon juice is a good natural bleach for stains on work surfaces, and raw onion will shine up baking pans.
- Cooking water from potatoes helps to remove the tarnish from silver cutlery, and Worcestershire sauce or lemon juice and salt will clean brass.
- Clean limescale in toilets with flour and vinegar which is left to soak, then removed with a brush. The acid in flat cola drinks also cleans. Use tea tree oil to disinfect the toilet bowl.
- Use dried herbs as an air freshener. Fill a bowl with rose petals and leaves and toss in citrus oil; put a favorite essential oil in an atomizer/mister with water and spray around the room.
- Kaolin (china clay) or fuller's earth and mixed salt and bran make good upholstery and carpet cleaners. Make a thick paste with water and leave on for 24 hours if stains are oily.
- Deodorize carpets by sprinkling bicarbonate of soda for an hour and then vacuuming. For a pleasant smell, just add a few drops of essential oil to the soda.
- Remove red wine stains by sponging on some white wine vinegar, then rinsing with water.
- Cloves, dried mint, cayenne, and chilies keep away ants and mice.
- A few drops of tea tree oil on a dog or cat collar can help keep fleas at bay.

ABOVE Instead of chemical air fresheners, use dried herbs, such as lavender, in bowls or sachets. They are especially useful in the bedroom.

LEFT By-products from laundry detergents have accumulated over the last 50 years and there are researchers who believe these by-products actually mimic female hormones. The resulting pollution is therefore linked with a significant decrease in the male sperm count, which has been falling by 2 percent per year for the last 20 years.

- Vinegar makes a good fabric softener, and also helps to stop colors fading. You can also add bicarbonate of soda, oil of lemon and eucalyptus for a pleasant fragrance.
- Dried lavender can be boiled and the fragrant water can be added to the final rinse.
- Use a magnetic washball – the magnetism gives the water the ability to clean fabric without the need for detergent.

Natural cleansers
- Make good ecological, all-purpose cleansers from: distilled malt vinegar, bicarbonate of soda, lemon juice, and lavender oil.
- A child's marble placed in a kettle will help to combat limescale.
- Vinegar is a good, non-greasy window cleaner and a good stain remover.
- Lavender, tea tree, rosemary, and thyme oils all make good disinfectants and bactericides.

ABOVE This beautiful beam makes a stunning design feature in this living room – however, you should avoid being directly underneath it. Not all beams feel oppressive, but they do disturb the flow of energy, creating a pressure on those who sit directly below. Over time, this can lead to headaches, tiredness, anxiety, and even depression. Move the seat elsewhere, or use it for visitors who will only spend a short time there.

"The harder and more lifeless our surroundings, the more tired, tense, and sapped of life we tend to become. The softer and more alive they are, the more renewed, relaxed, and healed we tend to be..."
Christopher Day, author of *Places of the Soul*

Use good feng shui for a healthy environment

Environmental stress is caused by not following the good princips of feng shui, which is a simple understanding of how we are connected to, and influenced by, the environments in which we live and work. Adjusting the energy flow in our home and surrounding environment can help to create a healthier life.

Much of this knowledge, and the name by which it is best known, comes from China, but feng shui embodies principles used by many traditional communities. It does not necessarily require any belief system, since energy flows influence everything around us, but it does become more powerful when we work with its principles in a positive way. Feng shui dates back to the time when humans would seek shelter in a cave and choose the one that afforded the greatest protection. It was used prominently by Chinese emperors observing the movement of the sun, moon, and stars with complex tables of calculations that enabled them to decide how best to harness the natural flow of energy when creating buildings. The Balinese still build houses that base the design of the building on the actual measurements taken from the various parts of the body of the head of the household.

Today, we can benefit from the wisdom of feng shui by paying attention to how we arrange our homes, but we need to remember that much of the most relevant knowledge comes from within. We already know deep inside us when we are comfortable and secure, when a place feels healthy or not, but many of us have forgotten how to recognize and work with these feelings. Even the folklore of our grandparents would stand us in good stead for creating more harmonious living spaces. So what happened to that connection? Our lives have become more cluttered and this makes it more difficult for us to be able to listen to our inner voice. We need to ask more questions and listen to the response from our intuitive self.

Creating a healthy home

To ensure that your home has a healthy atmosphere, you need to increase your awareness of your surrounding environment so that you can check for good energy flow. If you have any "environmental stress" brought about by blocked energy, it will affect the quality of your life. The following key principles will support you in checking that your home has good feng shui and is not creating any stress for you.

Your home is a mirror of you

Take a look around and be objective about it. In feng shui we look at the home as the extension of the person. Everything about that place is a reflection of them or the people who live there. All their past experiences and current circumstances are held within it, as are all their future dreams. Each object has been chosen by the occupants for a reason. When you know how to "read" a home, you can get to know a great deal about the person. For example, items that are broken and waiting to be repaired can sometimes indicate that something in that person's life is broken and needs to be fixed.

When we are focusing on health, it is most important that everything about our homes is in good working order. Watch out for areas of distress and decay that occur, and don't leave them too long before you sort out the root cause and fix them.

Your front door

Your front door is the most important gateway to your home because it is here that energy finds a way in. This is what is called the "mouth of chi," or the gateway through which the life-enhancing energy from the outside will flow in. It is critical that this flow is not blocked, so you need to make sure the door can open fully, that there is nothing behind the door blocking the entrance, and that the area around it is not overgrown and is in good repair.

Whatever object the energy flows around will impregnate it and affects its quality. So common sense dictates that you should not allow this fresh energy from the outside to be tainted by dirt and dust and dampness from the walls of the hall. Make sure your hall is clean and fresh, and the energy will then remain strong and vital.

LEFT This hallway has been arranged so that there is plenty of space for energy and fresh air to flow in and circulate. The pale walls and table lamp keep the area bright and light, and the mirror expands the space to make it even more welcoming.

LEFT It can feel awkward to have a doorway that cannot be used because it is blocked. This ornamental chest is obstructing the way between two rooms, so it should be moved to maintain a flow of good energy. Removing physical obstructions can shift the life force in both your body and your life.

RIGHT Shape, light, and color all combine to create a positive atmosphere. Here the natural shape of the curve of this ceiling provides a space that is easier on the eye and more relaxing than the boxiness created by straight lines. Curves make the energy flow more easily, and help to make spaces feel more alive.

Your front door is also a vital connection to the outside world and, in a sense, particularly in terms of appearance, it represents how you will be seen and judged. What does it say about you? Is the area neat and tidy? Is the door tired looking, chipped, in need of repainting? Is it well kept, clean, and welcoming? Energy flow to our homes is also a metaphor for the flow of fortune that can come our way. If you want opportunity to knock on your door then you need to make sure you can be found easily. You need good lighting, a clearly displayed number or name, and a working bell or knocker. Very often people who lack clarity in their lives and cannot see their way forward will have dark, dingy entrances to their homes, with poor lighting or even no illumination at all. It is surprising how simple the metaphorical messages can be.

Well-balanced energy flow

Energy needs to be able to flow around the home easily and be able to reach every part of it. Once inside, energy will flow around your home and nourish every corner, provided it can get there. Make sure that it can do this.

Anywhere that is cluttered, where you feel cramped or blocked or find that you have to squeeze to get through, is a good indication of energy flow problems.

Avoid putting seats in corridors unless the access is very wide, since these will block easy movement. It is unlikely that anyone will want to sit there, and the chair will probably just accumulate clutter. If you create obstructions you will end up having to make up for the resulting awkwardness, and this is often indicative of compromises that we have to make in our lives. Narrow spaces can be made to feel bigger by bringing in extra lighting, painting the walls a light color, and even using mirrors to open up the space. Think how much smaller that tiny toilet cubicle on an airplane would seem without being paneled with mirrors.

Healthy plants help to bring in energy and keep it moving in the interior. The more plants you have around you, the more vibrant the energy will be moving around your home. The next chapter considers the vital contribution that plants in your home can make to your well-being (see page 98).

TOP AND RIGHT Make sure the area between rooms is unrestricted. The top picture directs the energy within the space, whereas in the right-hand one it is blocked.

CENTER The profusion of colors makes this bathroom a fun and quirky space, but it would be hard to find anywhere else in the home where this would feel comfortable.

Obstructions to energy

Heavy furniture in awkward places impedes the flow of energy, so you may need to rearrange it. Try not to have too much in a small room. If a room is filled with furniture then there will be hardly any space left for the energy to flow through freely.

Different colors also affect the flow. Dark, heavy colors such as deep burgundy or brown/black can slow it down, while lighter colors like whites and creams reflect the light and help to create more movement. The next chapter (see pages 112–127) explores further how you can use different colors to create different feelings in a space depending on how you want to use a room.

A healthy flow of energy should not be too fast or too slow. Long corridors tend to speed up energy flow, and this can be particularly disturbing in a home if the long corridor is situated between the front door and back door. It is as if the energy that comes in through the front door can see its fastest escape route at the back of the house and goes there immediately, without nourishing the home along the way. You can slow this down by placing items to moderate its flow, such as windchimes, plants, narrow side tables, pictures, and lights.

Avoid uncomfortable energy

The natural world is full of curves and flowing lines, and energy will naturally follow these contours. Sharp corners and angles in the interior will disturb the smooth flow of invisible energy. Imagine sitting at a square table for four, not at a smooth side but at a corner with the sharp edge facing you. It would feel extremely uncomfortable and you would not want to stay there for very long, not because the sharp edge was actually touching you, but because of the force field of energy directed towards you from that point.

So avoid placing objects with square corners very near to places where people will sit or sleep. Another design feature that can create uncomfortable energy is a ceiling beam, often made from attractive dark oak in older properties. When this protrudes from the flush ceiling, it disturbs the smooth energy flow, causing a ripple effect of pressure below it. This can cause illness if the beam is sited directly above where someone regularly sits for long periods of time or sleeps all night. If this is the case, remove the chair or bed away from under the beam to avoid the effect.

The effects of clashing colors

Each color has different qualities associated with it and affects our moods and feelings. Some combinations of colors naturally go well together, while others can feel discordant. Take care not to bring too many colors into a room since this can confuse the energy and end up being too stimulating. The same principle goes for patterns and designs. While some rooms can look interesting with an unusual combination of different designs or an eclectic collection of varied styles, take care not to have too many patterns. They might clash and this can overwhelm the senses, making a room feel stressful. There is a point beyond which a room stops being interesting or entertaining and ends up being very distracting to all the senses.

Powerful symbols

Symbols are the language of the subconscious mind; they help us to understand the world we live in. Our homes are full of symbols and

metaphors, and very often we choose them without thinking about them consciously. They can be enormously powerful. Spiritual leaders in the past have communicated their teachings through stories and parables in which people could recognize themselves. The ideas were not only passed on orally but also through art in pictures. When we choose a piece of art we may be attracted to it because of its style and color, but there is also something about the image with which we feel comfortable. We select it because it is reinforcing some belief or feeling that is deep within our subconscious. When we make conscious choices in art we can surround ourselves with symbols that positively reinforce some aspect of our life or ambitions. The easiest way to understand this is that many people who live alone often choose pictures of lone people. It either reinforces what is happening in their life or expresses their need for a more single life. When single people are actively looking for a partner they should review the symbols that they have in their home and change them to include more paired images or pictures of couples. This ensures that their environment is aligned with their desire for a relationship.

RIGHT The large windows will make anyone sitting in the chairs with their backs to the window feel vulnerable, and they will find it difficult to relax. Placing low, heavy furniture in the window, or even bringing in large plants, will help contain the energy in the room.

A feeling of protection

One of the most basic principles of feng shui is to choose a protected site on which to build your home. Traditionally, this would have meant having the protection of a mountain or hill behind it to shelter your home from the cold northern winds, while having an open aspect to the warmer southern sun in front. Being close to water, necessary for all life, would also have been a significant factor, and ideally this water source would have been flowing in front of your property and not behind it.

Of course, very few of us, today, have the luxury of choosing such protected locations for our homes since most now live in either apartment blocks or ready-built houses, but the principle of feeling safe and protected remains the same. Even if we do not have a mountain (or tall supporting structure) behind our home, we can ensure that our favorite chair, work desk, and our bed all have the support of a solid wall behind, while in front there is a clear view of what may come towards us. This important arrangement in a space simply gives you a feeling of security, to know that your back is protected, and that you can see what is going on in front of you and be prepared for it.

Mixing energies

The lack of space in most people's homes means that some rooms might have a dual purpose. A bedroom may also be used as a work space, or a living room may also double as the children's playroom. We function most effectively, however, when the space we are in is designed to support what we are doing. We sleep much better when our bedroom is designed to be peaceful and calm. Unfortunately, this environment does not necessarily support

the totally different function of work, where we have to be animated, clear thinking, and focused. If the environment is changed so that it can more effectively support this daytime activity, it is more than likely that the room will no longer be a haven for sleep since the two very different sorts of energy will not mix well together.

If the bedroom must have dual work/sleep functions, it is a good idea to screen off the bed area during the day and the work area at night. Have different lighting systems so that you can work with efficient desk lighting during the day and switch on softer, more calming and soporific lights at night in order to change the mood of the space and signal to your body that the business day is over and that it is time to switch off, calm down, and relax.

ABOVE Whenever possible, avoid bringing your work into your sleeping space, especially if you can still see it from your bed. Being reminded of work just before going to sleep can create an underlying anxiety and affect the quality of your sleep. Put it away or hide it by placing a screen in front of it.

Light

"Where the sun does not enter,
the doctor does."
Italian proverb

Over the centuries our bodies have adapted to the cycles of the sun, and our biological clocks follow the cycles of light and dark. Natural light not only nourishes our physical wellbeing, but a lack of it can severely affect our psychological and emotional balance. Around 10–11 percent of the British and American population are estimated to suffer from Seasonal Affective Disorder (SAD) during the winter months, which makes people lethargic, depressed, gain weight, and crave carbohydrates and can even drive some sufferers to suicide.

RIGHT Natural light gives life and atmosphere to a room. Here the patches of sunlight and patterns caused by the light flooding in through the shutters create a breathtaking beauty in the room, and have more impact than anything we can create with decorations.

LEFT The more time you spend indoors, then the more important it is to find places where you can enjoy natural light. Having access to daylight not only improves people's psychological well-being, but also helps the body's internal clock to run smoothly.

Light through history

The Romans understood the value of light and created buildings that took advantage of it. During the 1,000-year period up to the Victorian era in the 19th century, the health benefits of light were not taken into account. It was only when doctors discovered in the latter part of the 19th century that sunlight could actually kill bacteria, including the one causing tuberculosis (a major killer of the time,) that light was recognized as an important nutrient and contributor to good health. In the early 20th century, the dark, unlit buildings favored by the Victorians were replaced by ones where good ventilation and sunlight were considered real priorities. Unfortunately, this eventually led to new building practices in the 1960s, which promoted office buildings that relied on air-conditioning and artificial light.

Light and moods

Looking at the sky, natural light and sunlight all powerfully influence our moods. The less light that is visible, the more stressed, trapped, and

depressed many people can feel. Shops that depend upon impulse purchases do better when sited on the sunny side of the street since people are more inclined to enter.

Dr. John Ott, a pioneering researcher into lighting and the effect on health, says that artificial light lacks essential wavelengths. People are now spending 75–90 percent of their time indoors, so it is important that buildings offer people some access to natural light. We can then experience the natural light of the seasons differently. In summer, with the longer daylight hours, we are energized by the light that enters our homes; while in winter, the shorter days and weaker light tends to slow us down and awaken our inner world, encouraging us to withdraw in the same way that other animals hibernate.

Windows allow us to maintain a connection with the cycles of the natural world outside, as we exist in an artificially controlled environment. Studies have shown that patients with a view out of a hospital window tend to recover more quickly and need fewer painkilling drugs. Many elderly people in nursing homes have been found to be deficient in vitamin D because they are not able to get outdoors. Indoor light, with its lack of ultraviolet radiation, impairs the intestine's ability to absorb calcium so that bone fractures are more likely when older people fall.

Windowless classrooms have been found to have a damaging effect on children's health and behavior. Experiments with rats and rabbits kept in windowless rooms showed that they attack each other and themselves.

The quality of light
Light will always give life to a room, but the quality of that light is more important than quantity. Just imagine the warm atmosphere

ABOVE Where the natural light is subdued, artificial lighting may be needed to enhance the level of illumination. When lighting levels are low, so is our energy.

LEFT Corridors can be dull spaces which take us from A to B. These glass doors allow in light to make this semi-outside area come alive. They also act as a useful transition space between living areas.

created by a single candle compared to the stark, unfriendly brightness of a single light bulb. Natural light has the full spectrum of light waves, which are ever-adapting alongside the time of day or season, whereas artificial light has the same pattern of mechanical fluctuations which are unvarying.

Bright sunlight can cause overheating and fading of materials. Daylight, however, is more diffuse and has a less drastic effect, including light from the sun and light from the sky. Our homes and work places need a balance of different kinds of light.

Daylight helps to regulate the body's internal clock, which in turn controls temperature and our sleeping/waking cycles. Sitting in a bright, artificially lit room for an evening means that our body can disconnect with the rhythms of nature and not always know that it is the right time to produce the sleep hormone, melatonin. This can artificially stimulate the body and make it more difficult to sleep.

Choosing lighting

Light creates brightness and life inside buildings. Choosing the right lighting can make an enormous contribution not only to your physical and mental health, but also to your social well-being. Working under bright, artificial light all day long can make you feel ill and tired, so it is important to counteract this with the right level and type of illumination, as well as making sure that you go outside for a while in the natural daylight every day.

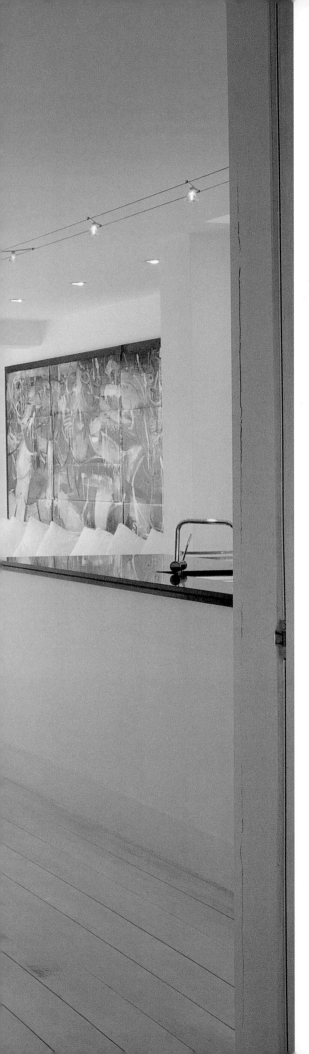

Most rooms need good general lighting to give overall illumination, as well as task lighting so that you have good light when you are sitting down reading, for example. General lights should have a dimmer switch, since these allow more flexibility as to which mood you want to create. There are several different types of light bulbs that are used in the home, and they need to be selected carefully.

Conventional incandescent light bulbs

These are the safest and most popular choice as they produce very small electromagnetic fields and light up instantly, with no flickering, giving a warm, healthy glow. However, incandescent light bulbs contain no ultraviolet rays, which are essential for good health.

Daylight versions can be purchased that use different colors in the glass to change the light to something nearer daylight. This can prove very effective in changing the mood of a room with color – for example, a blue hue is cooling and calming, a pink light is warming and cozy, and an orange glow gives an uplifting mood.

Fluorescent lighting

These artifical lights are much more popular in work places than the average home, but people do use fluorescent lights, especially in kitchens and in laundry and utility rooms.

They have been particularly favored in public places because they create an overall light without shadows, consume less electricity, and can last up to six times longer than incandescent bulbs. However, they are not a restful light and can cause excessive fatigue, irritability, eyestrain and headaches, partly because of the sub-perceptual flicker and also due to the enormous number of positive ions they produce, which

Healthy lighting tips

- *Be creative with how you place lighting, and use it to create a mood.*
- *Use full-spectrum light bulbs to emulate natural light in work areas, kitchens, and bathrooms.*
- *Check that all bulbs have shades.*
- *Be more creative than just having a central light. There are three types of lighting: general, task, and atmosphere. Most rooms need all three. Use uplighters, downlighters, table lamps, and floor lamps.*
- *Natural lights, such as oil lamps and candles, bring a lovely, soft glow to a room, but never leave them unattended.*
- *Create different levels of lighting; don't have all rooms with the same levels of brightness.*
- *Use light to illuminate dark corners. Light is energy, and it helps to avoid stagnation when it reaches into the far-off parts of a room.*
- *Not everywhere needs to be illuminated. Some corners may benefit from being left as cozy spaces where people feel safe and protected.*

create tiring and stressful environments. Research by American scientist Dr. John Ott has linked bad behavior in schools with this type of lighting.

There are many scientific studies which have also demonstrated that these lights can have carcinogenic effects. This is partly because some of them still contain the known carcinogen PCB (polychlorinated biphenyls) in the ballast that provides the starting voltage. These lights have also been associated with the increased number of cases of cataracts, melanoma, allergies, and ADD (Attention Deficit Disorder), which occurs in children.

Fluorescent lights create a background hum and, more worryingly, give off higher levels of electromagnetic radiation, which the London Hazard Centre says is enough to have an adverse affect on the nervous and reproductive systems. It identified the following symptoms and diseases known to be linked to exposure to fluorescent lighting:

- *Hyperactivity and other mild behavioral disorders are linked to flickering.*
- *There is an increased risk to epilepsy sufferers.*
- *The aging of the retina is speeded up.*
- *A higher incidence of miscarriage.*
- *There is a link to skin cancer. A study of more than 800 Caucasian women workers in England and Australia showed that exposure to fluorescent lighting at work may double the chances of developing melanoma.*

More modern fittings tend to use an electronic ballast to start the light so that they no longer have a flicker and give off significantly fewer EMFs.

The cathode tube contained in fluorescent lights must have a protective cover as it emits x-rays. If you have a broken one, always replace it for health reasons, not just aesthetic ones.

Natural daylight bulbs

These are closer to natural daylight, and give a clearer illumination that is better for reading. They contain a blue light not present in incandescent bulbs, so while the light may seem colder, it is actually better for the eyes.

Full spectrum lights

Full spectrum lights replicate the full spectrum of the light waves that appear in daylight, and give off a bright light. They are only available as fluorescent strips.

Their unique coating results in a light that is remarkably close to sunlight, enabling people to survive better in artificial environments. They are particularly helpful for sufferers of Seasonal Adjustment Disorder (SAD).

Full spectrum lights contain ultraviolet light (UV) waves to which our bodies are attuned. These waves are important to health as they can lower blood pressure and increase brain activity, which improves work efficiency and decreases fatigue. Ultraviolet light is vital for good health in small doses, but in large doses it causes sunburn and can lead to skin cancer. Choose a polarizing filter that stops glare and makes the light appear more like natural daylight from the north.

Energy-saving lights

These are mini-fluorescent tubes and may have a small EM field. They save energy, have a high output of light, and use a modern electronic ballast, so that flickering is not a problem.

Halogen lights

These are small bulbs which provide a bright incandescent light that is far more intense than ordinary bulbs. The light they give is closer to daylight, but they also emit intense heat so they need special light sockets and some shielding. Halogen lights also need a transformer, which produces high electromagnetic fields, so before having them installed, work out whether these transformers can be sited away from seating and sleeping areas. You also want to avoid siting them in a ceiling that is also the floor of a bedroom.

The other concern is their potential as a fire hazard, providing roughly five to ten times the power of the equivalent incandescent type of light bulb. Make sure that moveable ones are positioned well away from flammable material.

GEOPATHIC STRESS

ABOVE LEFT If a cat is regularly drawn to a particular area, this can be an indicator of a line of geopathic stress. A half-finished job is also an indication of a household drained of energy by geopathic stress.

ABOVE RIGHT A dilapidated house in an otherwise well-kept neighborhood is a sign that a property is riddled with GS, making the owners feel tired and unable to gather together the energy to maintain the property.

Our ancient ancestors lived in a world where they were in harmony with the natural rhythms of the earth. They did not suffer from the effects of artificial radiation and were therefore sensitive to the fact that life flourished in some places, while in others animals became sick and vegetation did not thrive. They learnt to avoid less healthy areas, and worked out how to change an area from negative to positive by the way they related to it in ritual and ceremony.

In the modern world it seems that this way of relating to earth energies has been forgotten as buildings are erected over mine shafts, underground cavities, fault lines, and running water, all of which create distortions of energy.

The ancient people's understanding and skills needed to clear or avoid geopathic stress are more important today than ever before. If they felt unwell they believed that they could heal the unnatural earth rhythms by using time-tested rituals. They also created systems of standing stones and sacred monuments to maintain energy balance.

What causes geopathic stress?

The term geopathic stress (GS) comes from the Greek "geo" (earth) and "pathos" (make sick) and means disease from the earth. It is the name used for distorted or unstable electromagnetic fields coming from the earth. These natural energy fields under the ground are changed by something that creates a discordant resonance above the ground. This invisible energy then "appears" as a line or ray of geopathic stress, which is typically about a foot or so wide. Where there are serious disturbances of energy, they can be as large as the width of a house, but this is extreme.

The negative effect of GS lines can be felt as strongly on the 20th floor of a building as on the ground floor, because the amount of concrete and steel used in modern construction amplifies the negative earth radiations.

Underground water can carry the vibrations of GS, amplifying the negativity, so water that flows under a home can prove harmful to its occupants. Natural earth movements can create friction where there are large mineral deposits and faults in the substrata, and these are all natural sources of GS.

However, there are an increasing number of man-made causes. Large movements of earth and rock and deep excavation work for mines, quarries, roads, railway cuttings, underground trains, electricity pylons, and building foundations can all bring about the discordance that is known as GS.

It is important for people to check for geopathic stress in the home, and either to move furniture to avoid negative areas or to use electrical devices or other methods to neutralize it, so that the effects of this bad energy does not prove detrimental to health.

The effects of GS

The harmful influence of GS can be found in many homes today. It is on the increase because it appears that it is boosted by electromagnetic pollution from electrical appliances and supply lines. GS is most harmful if a line "appears" in your bedroom crossing your bed, or even worse if two lines cross each other. The effects are felt strongly because you spend seven to eight hours sleeping in that one place so your whole body is affected, and for some reason the radiations from the earth have been found to be stronger at night. So instead of your body being nourished by the earth's natural frequency, it is bathed in another frequency that does not support the proper functioning of the body. This causes disturbance of the immune system, and many different symptoms can appear that have now become associated with GS. Because of the general energy disturbance, people who live in geopathically stressed homes are also more likely to argue, suffer from financial problems, lack energy, vitality and concentration, and experience bad luck.

Mental and emotional upsets

The Dulwich Health Society in Britain claims to have dowsed the houses of many families where the occupants have divorced or had cancer, and its research shows that 95 percent of these homes were affected by GS. If your home is fine, but you are sitting on a GS line during the day at the office, this is no better. Offices with lines that run through particular desks will have a higher level of illness, absenteeism, and low morale for those employees. If you find it hard to concentrate or stay awake in certain rooms or places, you can be reasonably sure that GS is present there.

ABOVE LEFT AND RIGHT

A gnarled or twisted tree is usually a sign that there is a geopathic stress line underneath it. Prolific ivy growth, especially accompanied by building cracks, can be another signal.

This may make uncomfortable reading, but there is a huge amount of research and anecdotal evidence to substantiate the claims. One of the most well-known proponents of GS is Kathe Bachler, an Austrian teacher, who conducted research on 11,200 sleeping places earlier this century. She found that 95 percent of children with learning difficulties were found to be sleeping on GS lines. In European countries such as Austria, Germany, and Poland, people are much more aware of GS and many doctors actually send dowsers to check for it, if they suspect that their patients may be suffering from its effects.

Modern construction now takes place in almost any location because of land shortages, and areas that would previously have been thought unsuitable by traditional people are now being used. Also, many modern building materials have the potential to amplify any negative radiations that are already there.

Sensitivity to GS

People can be very sensitive to the effects of GS and will often unconsciously feel its "vibrations" when they enter a building for the first time, although they may not understand that this comes from GS. So houses with geopathic stress do not sell easily, and businesses that offer a public service, such as restaurants, shops, and hotels, do not seem so appealing to people when they are affected by GS.

Geopathic stress may well be harmful to humans, but some animals thrive on it. Dogs are very disturbed by its effects and will never settle if their basket is unwittingly placed in a GS zone, but cats love it and can sometimes be a good indicator of the stress. Watch out for their favorite sleeping places and test them, especially if they all line up throughout the house. Ants and wasps are attracted to this energy, so nests can also indicate a GS zone. Once a line of GS is cleared, you will probably see that the ants will disappear. If for any reason the stress returns, so will the ants.

If you have a GS line running through your home you may well see the line winding its way through the yard, and where it lies under a hedge there is likely to be a gap there where the vegetation does not grow well. Trees can also be seen to develop cancerous growths and nodules and twist their trunks more. Damp, mold, and cold patches are also prevalent in these areas.

GS areas also have stagnant energy, attracting clutter, cracks in the plaster, and broken windows and paving slabs. In addition to the noticeable physical signs, you may also feel very tired or uncomfortable in a certain part of a room. A home that looks neglected is a sure sign of a building riddled with GS, where the occupants battle against lethargy to try to keep up with the repairs that seem to be constantly needed.

It is not always possible to spot all the signs of GS, but you can check by dowsing, that is by tuning into the vibrations under your home using a dowsing tool. See pages 64–65 for a step-by-step guide to trying out the dowsing technique for yourself.

Dealing with geopathic stress

One simple and immediate solution if you have geopathic stress in your home is to move your chair, relocate your bed, or move to another bedroom. Always try to avoid sleeping or spending long periods of time on GS lines in the first place. Most houses which have GS in one area, have another place that is safe – a solution can always be worked out.

Clearing geopathic stress

A line of GS located through a hall or corridor, for example, does not threaten your health in the same way as a line running through your bed, your favorite chair or your stove or oven. Cleaning it generally involves some kind of expertise, so it is better to find an expert dowser or a trained feng shui professional. They should know exactly where to work, and can change or harmonize the resonance of the GS line with the use of a technique called earth acupuncture (visit www.thehealthyhome.com.) for a register of trained practitioners).

Neutralizing any bad energy

Electrical devices can be purchased that emit various signals that change the vibration of the distorted energy. The Dulwich Health Society in the UK produces a Raditech machine that simply plugs into an electrical socket. Another plug-in device is the much-rated Helios 1 from Poland, which harmonizes GS by sending out emissions that are similar to natural earth energies, creating a harmonized and undisturbed environment throughout the rooms around it.

BELOW Various gadgets can be purchased to harmonize the energy in a space. This Helios simply plugs into the electrical circuit and helps to neutralize harmful radiations.

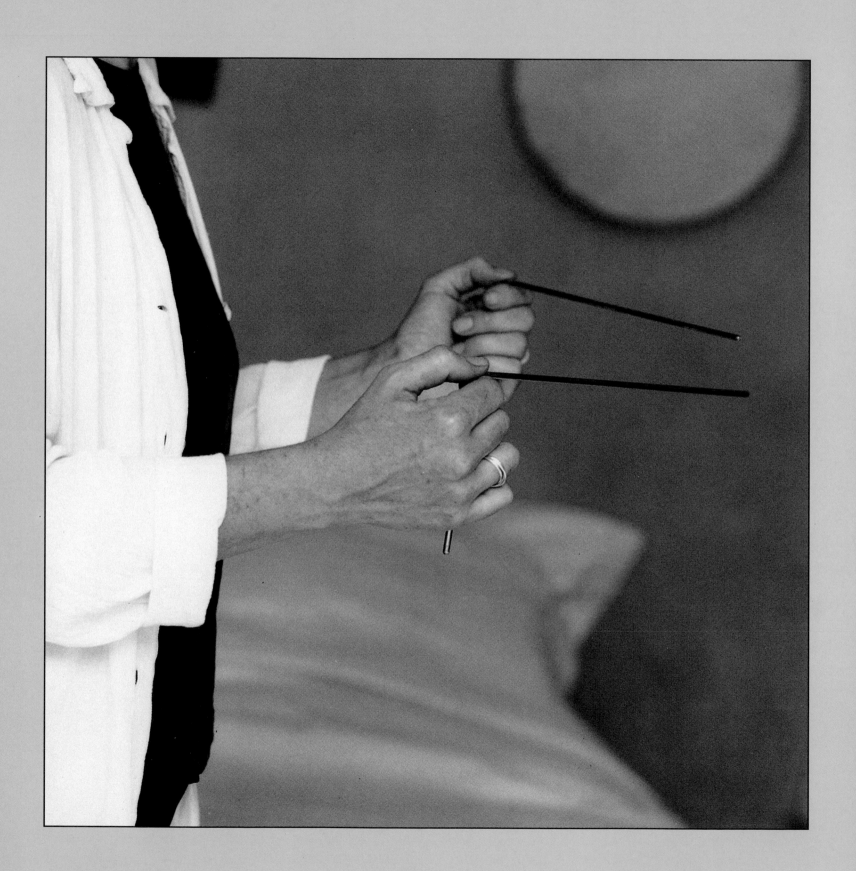

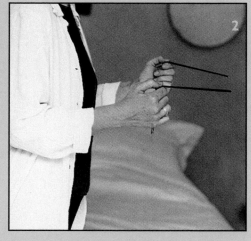

Dowsing for geopathic stress

It is not always possible to interpret all the signs, but you can check evidence of geopathic stress by dowsing – tuning into the vibrations under your home using a dowsing tool. Dowsing is a skill that some people have practiced and refined to an expert level, but everybody has the ability to dowse. Success depends on your willingness to learn the techniques and to develop your ability to focus on the process. You should use your intuition to help tune into the vibration of everything around you and start to interpret the reaction in your body. The process of dowsing is about feeling your way into the answers and setting aside the logical mind. Experienced dowsers use their own bodies, as it is the most sensitive dowsing tool, but it is best to start off by using a dowsing tool like a pendulum (anything that swings on a chain, thread, or string) or a pair of rods.

Simple steps for dowsing using rods

Copper L-shaped dowsing rods are used by many experienced dowsers since they are the most sensitive. However, if you find these hard to get hold of, you can make your own from two wire coathangers.

1 First survey the house or property. Start with anywhere that feels uncomfortable or that looks neglected before working your way through the other rooms in the house. GS lines in a hallway pose a less serious challenge to your health than those across your bed.

2 Prepare yourself mentally. Clear your mind and then concentrate on the following questions. Do I have permission to dowse? May I ask questions? Is it appropriate for me to dowse now? On your first attempt, it may seem that no response comes into your mind, however, unless you get a definite NO response, proceed.

3 Hold a dowsing rod in each hand and at chest height, with your arms shoulder-width apart. Your grip should be firm, but loose enough to enable the rods to turn in your hands to register a response. The rods will respond to any question requiring a YES/NO answer. Practice first over something that will contain GS, for example an ironwork bed frame or electric plug socket.

4 Relax and take several deep breaths. Start to walk across the room asking yourself the following questions: Where is there a line of geopathic stress? Please show me by crossing (Fig 1).

5 As you meet the line of geopathic stress the rods will start to cross (Fig 2).

6 When you are standing right on the line the rods will cross completely (Fig 3).

Check www.thehealthyhome.com for details of a dowser or where you can learn to dowse.

Our bodies are made up of the energetic systems of our mind, body, emotions, and spirit, and all of these are delicately interwoven and connected. When one of these systems gets out of balance, it eventually affects all the others. So if we regularly suffer from anxieties or emotional crises, they can eventually start to erode our physical health. Our immune system is not only weakened by the onslaught from increased toxins in our environment and in our food (see page 74), but also our ability to cope with that influx is diminished by the huge rise in the emotional toxins we create inside us from being anxious. Psychological and emotional pressures that affect us come from two sources: external factors in our life and our standard of living; and second, the degree to which we cope with demands and how we manage our emotions. Both relate to good health and may determine whether we will suffer from disease.

External pressures

Many people lead frantic lives in the fast lane – they work long hours and put themselves under huge amounts of stress. It has been shown that people are twice as likely to get a cold or develop an allergic condition if they are working under prolonged stress. A survey of British workers, published in the *Daily Mail* in 1999, found that 71 percent were stressed by the fast pace of their lives, while 40 percent stated that the time they took off work for sickness was directly caused by the stress being experienced.

In today's world, many people feel great pressure to work long hours in competitive high performance environments to achieve success. But what is our definition of success? In the West it is very much linked to having power, status, and material wealth, to live well with every creature comfort. And yet this is a very narrow definition of success, and one which is difficult to substantiate. A survey in 1998 by Demos, a British think-tank, suggested that money cannot buy you happiness. The research into the link between personal spending power and perceived quality of life showed that people in Bangladesh, one of the poorest countries in the world, got more happiness from their small incomes than the British do from their relatively large ones. In a league table of 54 countries, Britain ranked 32nd while the US managed 46th, with Bangladesh at number one. While the British had financial wealth compared to many countries, the report concluded that many people suffered from emotional poverty caused by consumerism and the breakdown of extended family and community life.

It is not the stress of change in our working lives, but the feeling of having no control over our workload seems to be the key factor in the stress chemicals in our body getting so out of balance that they can bring about illness. Where people are open to change and feel involved in the process, particularly at work, then the stress has no power to trigger disease. A feeling of helplessness has a debilitating effect on the immune system's ability to cope. People who stay healthier are those who can deal positively with change. Research among American managers showed that those who considered change to be an opportunity to grow and have a new experience tended to stay healthy, whereas those who felt it to be a threat to their security were the ones who became ill.

Achieving success is not just about material wealth or career development, but having all areas of our life in balance. With over-burdened and over-scheduled lives it is increasingly common for people to question the price they pay for achievement and to feel undervalued. Many people are not feeling valued at work and consider that the success they have attained is hollow. The ongoing stress of being discontented and dissatisfied with work, and having low morale, is now maintained to be a precursor of disease. According to a 1998 survey published in *The Globe* and *Daily Mail*, an incredible 80 percent of Americans have been found to hate

ABOVE People have always dealt with a variety of stresses. Today, people are away from their families for far longer and many suffer the daily discomfort of commuting, and yet it is the diminishing of our ability to cope that is more of a problem than the actual sources of stress.

LEFT In Spring 2000 the British government launched an initiative to encourage people to stop working so much and to invest in their home life. This concept originated in the US, and is founded on the belief that when workers have a good home life, they have less time off ill. Working longer does not mean working more efficiently.

ABOVE The change in family life since the 1960s has been dramatic. Routines have been dismantled and many families are now far less likely to get together for a meal.

ABOVE RIGHT Most women now work outside the home. Juggling different responsibilities can be very stressful, so it is important to try to find some time for yourself.

their job, and there also seem to be deeper spiritual issues at play. A survey published in *USA Today* noted that if a supreme being from a higher realm came to earth, the most popular question that 34 percent of people would ask was "What is my purpose here?" While the main concern of most under-developed nations is food, in the more developed cultures the main needs are a focused direction in life – namely a hunger for love, truth, purpose, and inner peace.

The cost of monetary success contributes significantly to daily stress. Traditional family life is being hugely disrupted by long working hours,

often for both partners, time spent commuting, and the pressure for many women to cope with work demands outside the home as well as nurturing the family. The traditional support systems are now breaking down, with families generally no longer having parents or extended family nearby to help out – is it any wonder that 40 percent of British marriages break down and end in divorce.

Emotional health

It is not just what happens around us, but it is our interpretation of events that can determine whether we get stressed. Our quality of health depends on how appropriately and effectively we react to the challenges that we experience.

In addition to our physical health, it is very clear that we need to take care of our emotional health. A minor illness can be a warning message from your body saying "Change what you are doing or how you are living". If such messages are ignored, a more serious illness can develop. People who live very stable, balanced lives with a good family and working environment seem to have an enhanced ability to repair their immune system. A US study published in the journal *Circulation* in 1997 showed a link between excessive mental stress and the narrowing of the arteries, resulting in damage similar to that done by cigarette smoking.

Our spiritual side is the inner voice inside us all that knows our truth, and knows what is right for us. It has an important role in helping us to create a balance in our lives, but many of us either ignore this intuition or do not have access to it because our stresses block us from hearing what it is saying. Anything that we can do to get in touch with our spiritual side will help to realign our lives and create good emotional health. One method is to ask yourself some empowering questions, such as: What if I were told I only had six months to live? How would I spend my time? Honest answers can help to put you back in touch with what you really feel are your priorities in life.

How to clear the mind

Feelings of anger, upset, fear, guilt, and resentment affect the levels of physical, cellular, and bio-chemical toxicity in our body. When our mental equilibrium is disturbed by anger the acid/alkaline balance of our body is swung towards acidity and our delicately tuned, life-maintaining processes must do what they can to restore a healthy alkaline environment to the body. If these floating acids cannot be easily expelled from our blood they have to be deposited elsewhere in the body, and this can bring about disease.

According to Caroline Myss in her book *The Creation of Health*, the root of ill-health and disease comes from eight dysfunctional patterns, which are:

• *Unresolved, deeply consuming emotional issues.*

• *Negative beliefs.*

• *An inability to receive love.*

• *A lack of humour.*

• *A need to control.*

• *Ignoring the physical needs of the body.*

• *A loss of meaning to life, feeling worthless.*

• *A tendency for denial (of any life issues).*

Living with a purpose

I think that fundamentally, there are two ways of living life. In the first instance we are continually being buffeted by the circumstances in which we find ourselves, resulting in a life path and situation outcomes that we do not plan and possibly do not really value.

The other way involves finding a real purpose for our lives, some guiding vision, which can draw us forward through life even in the face of inevitable difficulties, setbacks, and problems. When we are carried along by circumstances beyond our control, we make decisions from

what we have seen, heard, and experienced previously. We are then limited by our past and are unable to exercise free will.

When we are drawn forward by a vision of our future purpose, we, and our actions, own the future, so we are able to take control of our own destiny. This is our natural birthright as human beings, the ultimate expression of free will. So the choice is simple: you can own the future or you can be owned by the past.

When our lives reflect a higher spiritual purpose, the various mental toxins that consist of anger, distress, fear, guilt, and resentment are naturally dissolved by its power. As a result we are then free to achieve what we truly want and live our lives to the full. In fact, this means that life becomes far easier to deal with, and anything becomes possible to achieve.

Creating a treasure map

This exercise helps you to realize your goals, live your dreams, and create the happy and healthy life you deserve.

One of the things I have noticed about life in general is that it is often the case that we get the things on which we focus. The act of focusing, or giving attention to something, directs energy to it. If, for example, you constantly think of negative situations, then it is much more likely that you will attract them. If you regularly project towards more positive outcomes in your life, such as a promotion at work, increasing your circle of friends, or the realization of a family project, then it is much more likely that the circumstances and people that you need to realize a goal will magically happen.

So if you hold positive expectations for how you want your life to be, you are already a long way towards creating a happier, stress-free life. In fact, just thinking the right thoughts is 90 percent of what is required: concentrate on what you want, rather than what you do not. The creation of a "Treasure Map" is an extremely powerful tool for bringing about the life you want. Here is how to do it:

1 Decide on your goal

What is your dream? How would you like your life to be? Successful business-development author John Kalench, suggests that you ask yourself three questions:

a) *If I did not have to go to work for a living, then what would I do?*

b) *If I was given a million dollars, what would be the first thing that I would spend the money on (forget the bills)?*

c) *How would I live the rest of my life if I were only given six (healthy) months to live?*

Another powerful suggestion from author Stephen Covey is to take stock of your life, imagine your own funeral, and ask yourself how you would like to be remembered. It is most important for our spiritual health that our lives have meaning.

2 Make the goal more real

Once you have identified the things you want to happen, whether they are lifestyle changes or specific items such as having a new car, you need to verbalize them. Saying them and writing them down starts the process of releasing them from your imagination.

Visualizing your goal happening also helps, so picture in your mind actually driving the car or having the job you want, and you will feel more connected to it.

3 Create a visual picture of your goals

Expressing your aspirations in symbols and pictures helps to turn dreams and goals into reality. This means finding photographs, magazine cuttings, and items that reflect what you want. They can symbolize an idea: for example, a picture of a golden bowl may represent to you that your life is full of blessings. If you want a new car then get a photograph from the car showroom depicting the exact model in your chosen color.

4 Preparation

Gather all chosen images together and arrange them on a board or poster. As you review them all together it may also show you more about what is happening in your life, perhaps highlighting an area that is out of balance. Create an appealing montage, and paste everything together on the board.

The image shows a collage or "treasure map" containing various flowers, garden images, and words including: gardens, borders, makeovers, private paradise, Creativity, FRIENDS, leisure, Laughter, Play, Joy, Far from ordinary, Support, glow in the day, financial support...

LEFT Flick through magazines and color brochures to find positive and stimulating images that reflect the life you want. Be bold, and think the unthinkable.

ABOVE Once your poster or "treasure map" has been created, continue to give it your attention and energy by looking at it daily. Don't focus on *how* your goal will be achieved — just focus on what you want and let magical things start to happen.

5 Keep it in your sights

Looking at your poster or "Treasure Map" will help you to begin the next phase of your life with the end in mind. Choose a place to hang it where you can see it everyday. Connecting with it daily will give you a sense of purpose, and a boost of energy that will support you in moving your life in the direction you want.

6 The power of ritual

You can make this process of searching for the treasure in your life even more powerful if you have some sort of ceremony when you complete it. This simply means creating a special moment by lighting candles, placing flowers, or playing a special piece of music. You could make it a real occasion by enlisting a friend as a witness, then together toasting your future.

7 Other techniques

In addition to visualization techniques, you can use affirmations. These are positive statements of your intentions in the present tense that you repeat to yourself every day. A good example is "I am relaxed and have all the energy and time I need to do everything I want."

We are what we eat, so every time we eat something we are making an important health choice. Most people think they eat a reasonable diet, but many Western diets are inadequate and some people are actually malnourished. Many of the dietary practices that we have grown up with are now recognized as being major contributors to degenerative diseases. While the effects of poor diet may initially only show up as lack of energy, irritability, or mild allergies, in the longer term, the food we eat might be doing much more damage to our health.

It is hard to correct a lifetime of poor eating, but we urgently need to review the food we eat and adopt new practices that contribute more positively to our health.

Too much food

Put simply, Western societies consume too much food. Our calorie intake is up to three times as much as people in less-developed countries, many of whom also lead much more active lives.

Our bodies can become stressed from eating a lot, and often it is too much of the wrong food. Because our bodies are not gaining essential nutrients from the food we are eating, our stomachs send out "hungry" signals even after we have eaten far more, in terms of calories, than is good for us. The problem for us is that the food looks so good and tastes delicious, too.

Over a third of the adult population in the US are overweight. Obesity rates have increased by 30 percent just in the last decade and the condition is responsible for over 300,000 deaths a year in the US. Eating too much shortens our lives, as well as causing other problems, including low energy. By drastically cutting our calories, for example by half, to less than 2000 a day, we could significantly extend our life span.

High-fat diet

In our Western society, it is a straightforward fact that we consume too much fat. Some Western diets have fat levels as high as 35–45 percent, where nearer 10 percent is needed. Fat is a valuable energy source, but when eaten in excess it contributes to obesity, cardiovascular disease, hypertension, arteriosclerosis (diseased blood vessels leading to heart attacks and strokes), diabetes, and cancer.

Animal fat is more harmful to blood circulation and cholesterol levels than vegetable fats, which include olive oil, the staple of the healthier "Mediterranean" diet. A high fat intake will seriously overwork the body's digestive system, especially if it is added to an already unhealthy sedentary lifestyle.

Processed food and additives

Much of the food that we eat today is processed for convenience, with too many additives and too much salt, which is thought to increase blood pressure. Easy convenience foods are not so easy for the body to digest effectively. Ann Marie Colborn in her book *Food and Healing* estimates that there are between 5,000 and 7,000 chemicals still used in food to preserve it, and enhance its appearance, color, taste, texture, and aroma. They can adversely affect nutrients in the food and often include deodorants, dyes, bleaches, acidifiers, hydrolizers, sweeteners, and even disinfectants.

Refined foods have often been stripped of essential nutrients. When refined and polished, wheat and rice have the outer husks removed which actually contain the essential minerals needed to metabolize those very grains. When white rice and flour are eaten, valuable nutrients are stripped from the body to digest them.

RIGHT There is a price to pay for continually eating fried and fatty foods. Once the transitory pleasure passes, we realise that we are piling on the pounds. The National Audit office claims that Britain has now overtaken Germany as the fattest nation in Europe, while in the US a quarter of the population is deemed to be vastly overweight.

Consuming too much red meat

The modern Western diet contains far too much red meat. *The New England Journal of Medicine* reported in December 1990 on the largest study ever conducted into colon cancer, involving 88,000 women, at Brigham Women's Hospital in Boston. The conclusion was that the more red meat and animal fats eaten, the more likely colon cancer was to develop. It takes energy to break down meat to its various usable elements, energy that could be being utilized to equip the body against cancer.

Eating too much protein

Again, the modern Western diet contains too much protein. High-protein foods require higher levels of salt and other minerals to be broken down into their essential elements. The problem is, when not enough minerals are consumed, the body's own resources are plundered, in order to digest the protein.

Research also shows that high-protein diets cause higher acidity levels in the blood, which makes the blood dissolve more calcium from our bones. Throughout the world, the incidence of osteoporosis, the degenerative bone disease, is linked directly to protein intake, as quoted in *Diet for a New World* by John Robbins (1992). Lowering protein intake protects calcium levels, which are so important to healthy bones. The China Health project in 1988 studied 6,000 people and concluded that in China, where they derive 7 percent of protein from an animal source, they have four deaths per 1,000 from heart disease. In the UK where 70 per cent of protein comes from animals, there are 100 deaths per 1,000 from heart disease.

Overconsumption of dairy products

Our diet also contains too much dairy produce. The Western countries that consume the highest levels of dairy produce have the most osteoporosis sufferers, as it is linked with a high intake of protein, which pushes calcium out of the body. Calcium is not only in cow's milk — 10 times more can be found in sesame seeds and kelp seaweed, where it is also in a form that is more readily absorbed by humans. High consumption of dairy products has also been tentatively linked to female gynecological problems, such as tumors and cysts, and to the higher incidence of breast cancer.

Dairy products cause allergic reactions in many people, producing excess mucus that tends to line the membranes of the digestive system, impeding the absorption of essential nutrients. Many imbalances in the body, such as sinusitis, asthma, and eczema, can disappear in a couple of weeks when dairy products are removed from the diet.

Drinking too many stimulants

Caffeine is a powerful stimulant, and it is included in popular drinks such as tea, coffee, colas, and other soft drinks. On the positive side it increases brain activity, temporarily relieves tiredness, and makes you more alert, but on the down side it can make your heart beat faster, raise blood pressure, and put the body into a state of stress. Because it is a diuretic, it makes the kidneys work harder and increases the excretion of calcium from the bones. It is addictive, and many people can suffer from withdrawal symptoms, such as headaches, when they stop drinking coffee, tea, or cola. It's a good idea to try to reduce your intake slowly and drink more plain water or herbal teas.

Sugar in the diet

We eat too much sugar in our diet. Most is refined and it is found not only in candies, chocolates, and confectionery, but in many processed, canned, and frozen foods. Some breakfast cereals made from rice and wheat contain a staggering 50 percent sugar. Refined sugar enters the bloodstream quickly, putting the body into a state of shock. This provokes the stress response and insulin is pumped into the blood, reducing the body's glucose (blood "sugar") levels. This sudden drop can cause erratic behavior, emotional imbalance, and the classic mood swings. This is then followed by a desire for more sugar, hence its addictive nature. Sugar provides no nutritional value since the calories are empty of vitamins and minerals. Over-consumption can lead to obesity and a lower resistance to disease.

Children's bodies are more susceptible to sugar and can have dramatic hormonal reactions. The healthy alternative is to use more natural sweeteners such as honey, maple syrup, fruit juice and rice syrup, which release more slowly into the bloodstream. These don't have such an intense impact on the body as refined sugars, which include corn syrup, sucrose, dextrose, and fructose.

Microwave cooking

For thousands of years our ancestors cooked their food over fires. Microwave cooking is a new innovation that changes the energy structure of food, and our bodies have not yet adapted in the decades since they were introduced. A Swiss food scientist, Dr Hans Hertl, conducted tests in 1989 on the blood of a small group of people who had eaten a meal cooked in a microwave and found that their hemoglobin levels had dropped affecting the blood's ability to carry oxygen. The research was banned by the Swiss courts until the European Court of Human Rights allowed its publication in 1998.

The use of pesticides

Most of our fruit and vegetables are sprayed with over a billion gallons of chemicals a year to control pests and diseases and to maximize output. Children may ingest four times the adult dose of chemicals as their organs are less able to deal with toxins. Some Third World countries still use banned chemicals such as DDT, so they can still reach the Western world in the food they export to us. Unsprayed organic produce is now becoming a popular alternative today.

LEFT It looks delicious and many of us would find it hard to refuse such a sweet treat, even when we are full. NASA scientist Dr. William Grant conducted an independent study published in 2000 that concluded that excess refined sugar should be considered a health hazard. Caffeine gives us a temporary buzz but decreases long-term energy levels. Decaffeinated coffee is not the answer since the chemicals used to flush out the caffeine pose their own problems.

TWO

Stress-relieving Measures

Apart from finding ways of combating the seven stressors that pollute the body, we can also, in our water tank metaphor, turn on the spigot to reduce the stress level in the body, therefore undermining each stressor's ability to make our bodies imbalanced. This chapter looks at the various stress-relieving measures that are open to us. Each one has an effect on health, but the first three – sleep, diet and exercise – are the most important. The rest of the de-stressors will all make valuable contributions to the quality of your life and your ability to control your own health.

There are three key things that health experts say contribute to us staying healthy – these are good nutrition, regular exercise, and good-quality sleep. Most people know about the first two but very few people recognize how much sleep can contribute to our well-being. In fact, of the three it is undoubtedly the most important. Sleep is a great healer, yet research indicates that 50 percent of people sleep so little or so badly that it adversely affects their health. Many people do not realize that there is a problem with the quality and quantity of their sleep.

The benefits of sleep

A lack of good sleep is a major source of stress in itself, because when we are asleep the body processes many of the stresses that we experience during the day. So deep, healing sleep is what we all need every night to stay healthy. Sleep is not a luxury, but a necessity to keep us going. Not having enough good sleep actually holds the power to kill. Research carried out by William Dement in his book, *The Promise of Sleep*, indicates that 110 million Americans sleep badly, and it is estimated that between 10–30 percent of people in Britain also experience sleep problems. There are many reasons why we do not sleep well. First, our minds are still too occupied with worries and anxieties because we do not know how to let go; second, our bodies remain too tense because of lack of exercise and use of relaxation techniques in our daily routine; and third, because we do not make good sleep a priority, we do not create rooms that effectively support sleep.

Sleep is not simply a state of bodily rest, as the brain is more active then than it is during the day. It releases combinations of hormones that stimulate cell activity, particularly growth hormones in young children. Many electrical changes occur in the brain as it sends out messages to the body to organize repair and renewal. Thoughts and ideas from the day are processed, our memory and learning abilities are optimized, and dreams, which play a central role in the lives of traditional peoples, can give us messages and guidance from our spiritual nature.

There are different stages of sleep, and it is the fifth stage, REM (rapid eye movement) sleep, which is most important. This is when the brain is as active as if it were awake but paralyzes the body to keep it still. Any muscle tension disappears at this stage, and the sleeper becomes deeply relaxed. The brain values REM sleep more highly than non-REM sleep and it seems to be more important for the body's healing process. REM sleep does not happen immediately, but generally follows an hour of non-REM sleep. If you wake up in the night worrying, or suffering discomfort, cold, or needing to go to the bathroom, you may ultimately end up getting your eight hours of sleep, but the quality will be impaired as the brain will miss some of its valued REM sleep.

How much sleep is required

Most people need around seven to eight hours' sleep each night. The amount of sleep needed varies at different stages of life: babies sleep for most of the day, with about 50 percent of that time in REM sleep, whereas an adult will spend only 15–20 percent of their time in REM sleep. Two-year-olds need about 12 hours sleep with an afternoon nap on top, while young children and teenagers need about 10 hours. Sleep requirements tend to decline in adulthood, with older people needing one or two hours less a night.

RIGHT The key to a good night's sleep is to check that the environment in which you spend the most time is really supporting you. Check your bedroom for any lines of geopathic stress and test for high electromagnetic fields, particularly around your head.

ABOVE AND RIGHT Sleep can be encouraged through natural sleep stimulants, such as the scent of lavender, either in a herb pillow or in an oil burner, or by having a relaxing bath by candlelight and a cup of herbal tea. These relaxants will help release tension and make sleep come much more quickly.

Sleep deprivation

Our brain records how much sleep we get, so if we miss an hour a night during the working week, the brain registers that five hours of sleep have been missed by the weekend. It needs you to recoup sleep, but will allow your body to keep on going with less sleep, largely because of the adrenaline buzz from the stress-induced hormone and the stimulation of, for example, work. Take away that stimulation and you will start to become drowsy at quieter times of the day, and often while driving.

According to William Dement's research, 23 percent of people admit to having fallen asleep at the wheel, while 33 percent of traffic accidents are attributed to drowsiness. It becomes harder to concentrate and make decisions, and some people believe that for every hour of sleep you miss in a week, you drop one IQ point. Short-term memory becomes severely impaired and you can end up operating on auto-pilot. Sleep deprivation is the cause of some of the world's most notorious accidents, including the Exxon Valdez oil tanker spillage in 1989.

Evidence is also now emerging that the amount of sleep you get will have an effect on how long you live. A study in Finland indicated that male poor sleepers were 6½ times more likely to have health problems, while female poor sleepers were 3½ times more likely. Sleep deprivation also affects the performance of the immune system, which helps us fight disease. Our ability to maintain an effective defence system is severely diminished by lack of sleep. A study in the US found that people who regularly stayed up until 3am had a 30 percent decrease in the body's natural cells that protect us from cancer.

Sleeping sickness

Sleep apnea makes people wake up every few minutes gasping for air because they cannot breath properly. About 40 percent of Americans are estimated to suffer from this condition, although many people do not know as they cannot remember waking up. This condition puts a huge strain on the body, and 38,000 fatal heart attacks and strokes in the US each year are believed to be linked to the disorder. Loud snoring is believed to be a form of apnea.

Many people think that being run down, apathetic, and lethargic are part of the human condition caused by boring jobs, a heavy lunch, or a warm room, but, in actual fact, they often signal a severe lack of sleep. Healthy sleep refreshes us mentally, and helps us to prepare for each day. Sleep deprivation makes us edgy and irritable and even produces a greater propensity for anger and violence. We can overreact, get impatient, our vitality and coping skills drop, and we lose our creative abilities. Sleep is a vital natural medicine, and we need to take a full dose of it every night to stay fit and healthy.

How to sleep well

- *Avoid all stimulants late at night. This includes sugary foods and caffeine drinks such as coffee, tea, cocoa, and colas.*
- *Choose something uplifting to read before sleep, because the ideas that we take into our minds last thing at night program our sleep. Watching the news in bed, for example, can fill your mind with disturbing images.*
- *Get rid of busy thoughts by making a list of everything you have to do the next day, note the issues to be resolved, then let them go. Your mind can release it to your powerful subconscious to work on while you sleep.*
- *Meditate for 10 minutes. If you don't have a quiet area, just sit upright in bed. Breathe deeply and easily to release thoughts from your mind. Connecting with your inner spiritual self will help you to de-stress.*
- *A brisk evening walk can help to induce sleep, particularly if you spend most of the day sitting or are inactive.*
- *Keep away from strong lighting in the evening as this can block the body's ability to manufacture melatonin, the sleep-inducing hormone.*
- *Herbs such as lavender are relaxing and can help to make you feel sleepy. Use a few drops of lavender oil in water in an aromatherapy candle burner to fill the air with its relaxing aroma. Alternatively, place a couple of drops of lavender oil on the side of your pillow or on a handkerchief.*
- *Keep warm; use a hot water bottle if necessary. Sleep experts say that while your feet need to be warm, your head needs to be cool.*
- *Take an evening bath by candlelight since this helps to reduce body tension. Add a few drops of essential oils such as lavender, neroli, or geranium to the bath water.*

- *Try a mattress with magnets, which create an energy field around you similar to that of the earth's magnetic field. This can help to deepen sleep and improve its quality as we become reconnected with the natural energy of the earth.*
- *Change to an orthopedic shaped pillow to support your neck, particularly if you snore.*
- *Camomile tea can be an extremely relaxing drink, so have some just before bedtime to take your mind off the stresses of the day.*
- *The time before sleep is precious, so be gentle on yourself, do whatever it is that relaxes you, and then let go of the day. Affirm to yourself positively that all is well in your world.*

LEFT Overhead beams can disturb the energy flow over your bed. That uneven flow has been corrected here by creating a four-poster frame with a light material above the bed and directly over the sleepers.

FAR LEFT Choose natural material like cotton and linen to sleep on. Man-made materials like polyester/cotton mixes can be stressful on the skin because they amplify the EMFs around the body.

As was discussed in the previous chapter (see pages 74–77), some types of food can harm us, but others have the ability to heal as well. If we can harness this capacity, then we can begin to restore the balance of our body, mind, emotions and spirit.

Food can make a very important contribution to our good health. We are in control of what we eat, and how often. We can learn to interpret better what our body really needs and give it the right fuel so that we are not wasting energy by making it work hard on foods that are doing us harm. It is a powerful medicine that we can use to help get rid of some of the toxins that we are carrying. When we eat foods that really are life-enhancing, we feel happy, our minds are clearer, and uncomfortable symptoms start to leave us. It can help us get rid of our stress.

Healthy eating guidelines

Start to make changes to your diet now, but do it gradually. Introduce new things, such as wholegrains, to your current diet, rather than remove everything that you feel is unhealthy all at once. You will gradually lose your taste for the more harmful foods as you start to eat more natural unrefined foods. Start with a new breakfast of organic wholegrains and try adding some miso soup. Include more unrefined and unprocessed foods in your diet, and eat more complex carbohydrates such as brown rice, oats (oatmeal and granola), wholewheat bread and pasta.

A healthy diet means that you can reduce your intake of vitamin and mineral supplements. When vitamin C is taken out of the orange and put in a pill, it is being removed from a whole system that usually accompanies it. The body is not sure how to interpret the vitamin C in isolation and, detecting an imbalance of vitamin C, will start to get rid of it. Nature provides everything we need in the right proportion.

Eat with the seasons

When a fruit such as a pineapple naturally grows in a hot climate, it is to cool down the people who live there. When you are experiencing the effects of a colder climate, cooling down your body is the last thing required, so you are better with local root vegetables. It has been found that one-third of people report headaches after eating cold food like ice cream.

Eat natural and fresh foods

Buy organic crops that have been grown without harmful chemicals. They have a higher content of protein and vitamin C, and they taste better. Freshly cooked food retains its invisible chi or life force that is lost in freezing and preservation. Make sure you eat some raw vegetables every day, although this should be avoided if you have problems with digestion.

Get more protein from vegetables

The Framlington Heart Study, started in 1949, has been the longest ongoing investigation into heart disease and diet. Its director, Dr. Castelli, claims that vegetarians have the lowest coronary disease, have a fraction of the heart attack rate, have only 40 percent of the cancer rate, and outlive meat-eaters by an average of six years.

Change the balance of your diet

Aim to get 50–60 percent of carbohydrate intake from grains, 20–25 percent from vegetables, 5–10 percent from fruit, and the rest from unsaturated fats, seeds, and proteins from beans, legumes and tofu. Expand your choice of drinks beyond tea, coffee, and cola. There are many different herbal teas, most of which bring some kind of therapeutic relief. Drink plenty of filtered or bottled water to flush out your system. Take about a quart of water a day so that you do not overwork the kidneys.

Try to eat earlier

By eating earlier in the evening your system processes food faster, making you feel healthier and helps to keep your weight under control. By about 8pm your digestive system starts to shut down, and energy is deployed elsewhere for other functions, like repair work.

Take time to chew more

Digestion starts in the mouth – it is here that the saliva analyses the food that then goes to the stomach. It sends messages ahead so that the right enzymes are produced ready for the food that is on the way. When you eat slowly and are relaxed you begin to notice how your body reacts to certain foods, giving you an understanding of what suits you.

Appreciate your food

Take a moment before you start eating to reflect on how precious food is and how lucky we are to have an easy supply of it. Take a deep breath, relax

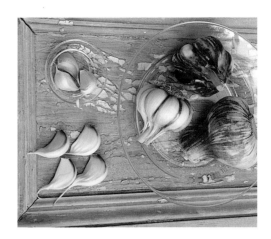

LEFT Choose local vegetables in season, and whenever possible buy organically grown ones as they are safer. Many of the vegetables bought in supermarkets have residues of pesticides. The World Health Organization estimates that there are 20,000 unintentional deaths a year from pesticides, mainly from organophosphates, which are widely used.

ABOVE Garlic's anti-bacterial, anti-fungal, anti-viral, and anti-parasitic properties have made it one of the most valuable remedies for colds and flu. It has an alkalizing effect, and also helps to regulate blood pressure. It is better when taken in natural form, rather than as pills. It is also a powerful antibiotic, and boosts activity of the immune system.

ABOVE A study by school caterers Gardner Merchant in 1999 found that one in four schoolchildren substitute their hot evening meal with sweet or spicy snacks. Left to their own devices, children will choose to eat highly processed foods. It is important for them to have a regular time to eat with the rest of the family.

RIGHT Miso is a paste of fermented soybeans, sea salt, and sometimes a grain like rice or barley. It is a great alkalizer, and can be made by simply dissolving the paste in water. Root vegetables can be added to flavor the broths as well as seaweed. Serve with chopped scallions and some tofu.

your body and mind, and concentrate on the taste of the food. John Robbins in his book *Diet for a New World* demonstrates that eating peacefully actually strengthens your immune system.

Fast to detox the system

When you go without food for at least 24 hours, your body diverts the vital energy that would have been used for digestion, assimilation, and elimination for deep internal cleansing. By only drinking water, you rid the body of toxins that can start to clog up the arteries. The longer the fast, then the deeper the cleansing. One day a week is great for stimulating regular repair and self-healing. A 7–10 day annual fast would make you more energetic and vibrant and is a great investment in longevity. Ensure that you check with a doctor before undertaking long fasts, and research exactly what and how much to drink to support your system over the fasting period.

Bring more balance into your diet

When we are ill it is our body's way of telling us that we need to make some kind of correction. Eating the right foods can help us to cope with a stressful environment, change our mood, and handle events appropriately.

Choosing the right kind of foods and then combining them properly is inevitably going to take some practice. Because food can play such an important role in keeping you healthy, make a point of finding the time to experiment with ways of integrating natural, unrefined, and unprocessed foods into your diet, especially macrobiotics. Such a diet will allow us to enjoy our old age to the full. Any extra effort and planning that might be required in the organization and preparation of an unrefined diet is an investment that will pay dividends.

Food can heal

Explore further the power of food as a medicine and a preventive measure. A British woman, Linda Kearns, has had recent newspaper coverage about a cake recipe that she developed that she believes can help rebalance women's bodies during the menopause, acting as an effective alternative to Hormone Replacement Therapy (HRT) drugs. In the process of her research into how other cultures coped with the menopause, she found that the Japanese did not even have a word for the hot flushes that seem to plague Western women. She attributes this to the fact that the Japanese diet is high in tofu and soy beans. Organic tofu has a good balance between protein and calcium and this, along with the soy flour, which is used in the cake.

After the atomic bomb was dropped on Nagasaki in 1945, both staff and patients at the hospital, just one mile from the center of the bomb, contracted radiation sickness. The director, Dr Akizuki, decided to feed everyone on a strict macrobiotic diet of brown rice, miso, wakame seaweed, and tamari soy sauce soup, with no sugar, and everyone survived, in contrast to others in the city who had developed radiation sickness. Miso, seaweed, and tofu are good for cleansing pollutants out of your blood. Seaweed, in particular, has the ability to crystallize radiation toxins, making it possible for the body to expel them easily.

EXERCISE

Regular exercise is one of the most important factors in maintaining a healthy body. And the less we take, the more it affects our bodies. It has been found that people who do not exercise regularly are more likely to die from heart disease, for instance.

A distinction also needs to be made between health and fitness. The people who put regular effort into becoming physically fit by working out at the gym or taking an active role in competitive sports (even professionally) can still suffer poor health from the effects of an inadequate diet, environmental and chemical pollution, and exposure to electromagnetic radiations. It is all about good balance.

The benefits of exercise

Taking regular exercise can have a great impact on your health, and can literally change your life forever. This will reduce the risk of heart disease, helps prevent osteoporosis, strengthens muscles, tendons and ligaments, and improves overall body image and self esteem. Here are four life-changing secrets about exercise.

LEFT Being indoors with central heating and artificial light can make you sluggish and lethargic. Just getting out into the fresh air can raise your levels of enthusiasm. Some people don't meditate because they find it hard to sit still, but a stroll can become a meditation, as you let yourself become aware of all your senses.

Exercise is great for weight loss
Exercising is the only really healthy way to lose weight. This is because when you exercise you increase the metabolic rate of your body, increasing the speed at which you burn up energy (calories).

If you exercise for a minimum of three times a week you will be burning food faster throughout the whole week. Simply reducing your food or calorie intake is not enough, because your body interprets the reduced intake of food as a signal that a famine is about to start and prepares to conserve fat – the very opposite of what you want – and gets rid of water and muscle instead. Everybody needs to exercise for good health, but many people also need it to lose weight.

Exercise helps stress and boosts physical health
Stress can affect our bodies adversely, because it creates chemicals that cause tension, making us feel irritable and on edge, always poised for action, and unable to sleep well. More worrying than that, stress diverts the body's resources away from the immune system's ability to repair cells and protect us from disease.

In a sedentary lifestyle, the stress hormone adrenaline builds up inside the body and can cause problems if it is not released. During exercise, adrenaline burns up, making it much easier to relax. People who exercise regularly have more efficient immune systems, so are less likely to become ill. If they do suffer a minor illness they tend to recover more quickly.

Exercise is good for us because it increases the strength and efficiency of the heart and lungs, develops stamina and muscle tone, and improves our digestive system and blood circulation, making our skin look healthier.

Exercise makes you feel better and boosts mental health

It can be a big effort to start exercising on a regular basis, but many people manage it and reap the physical and mental rewards, enjoying good fitness and increased happiness and vitality.

During a vigorous exercise session your body starts to produce endorphins, the "happy hormones" giving you an uplifting "high" which stays with you for several hours afterwards. Your whole body chemistry changes, giving you a feeling of peace and satisfaction. There is increased vitality and more energy to cope with life. This helps to get your life back into balance, and to enjoy your time with family and friends.

The vigorous oxygenation of the blood that occurs during exercise makes us feel brighter, happier, and more charged up and enthusiastic, with a greater mental clarity. When we are too inactive, we can feel lethargic, tired, depressed, lazy, and our outlook can be less optimistic.

Exercise is very effective in removing toxins

Vigorous exercise raises the temperature of the body tissues, warming up the blood, and helping it to circulate more efficiently. The result is that wastes and toxins that are deposited in the cells can be dissolved more easily in the warmer blood and washed away for removal by sweating, exhaling, or excretion. For this reason, it is important to drink plenty of water during and after exercise. In his special report on diet in January 2000, *Doctors Don't Tell You*, Dr. John Briffa says that the body is constantly working to eliminate the environmental pollutants that we absorb and eat. However, there comes a point when the body's normal cleansing system cannot keep up, so the toxins have to be stored out of the way. They like to lodge themselves in

the body's fat cells, and if we are not exercising enough and encouraging them to move out, our toxicity levels continue to rise and the body's back-up strategy seems to be to make the fat cells bigger to dilute the toxins. Remember that part of the aging process can be attributed to toxin build-up, so by releasing these toxins, you can find that you look years younger.

Choosing the right exercise

To get fit, you need to choose an exercise that will generate a sweat as it is the key to getting rid of toxins and acid wastes that build up and accumulate deep within the body. When the internal temperature of the body is elevated it expands the huge network of capillaries, enabling the warmer blood to reach the acid toxins piled up and so dissolve them. (Think how much easier it is to clean dirty dishes in warm water.) If you are not used to excercise and don't feel comfortable with the physical demands of working out or running, then don't underestimate the power and value of walking. One of the easiest activities to incorporate into your life, you can do it anywhere at any time, it requires no specialized knowledge or equipment, there is no risk of injury, and it can provide a total workout if brisk enough. You can even make the time productive if you carry a Walkman and listen to uplifting material or recorded books.

- *Find an exercise system that you enjoy, suits your personality and budget, and that you can do at least three times a week. Decide if you want your exercise to be social (aerobics, badminton, dancing) or solitary (weight training, walking, jogging, yoga).*
- *Regular exercise can improve your sense of well-being, and your sex life.*

- *Aerobic sports that work the heart and lungs include: cycling, jogging, running, skiing, dancing, swimming, circuit training, and tennis.*
- *Golf is very sociable, can improve muscle tone, and brisk walking on the course helps cardiovascular fitness. Jumping rope isn't just child's play; it provides a serious cardiovascular workout.*
- *Brisk walking of at least half an hour a day, five or six days a week, will improve your fitness. If you can't do this much, just take every opportunity to walk at a fast pace.*
- *More gentle forms of exercise use focused stretching movements and deep breathing techniques, like tai chi, qui gong, or yoga. They are suitable for all age groups, and work on both the body and mind, improving muscle tone and promoting relaxation, good concentration, and increased confidence.*
- *You can detoxify the body by raising the temperature with massage, having a sauna or hot bath; and using products with far Infrared technology.*
- *Change your exercise program with the seasons (make sure you get outside for at least half the year), get friends to support you, and keep looking until you find something that really works for you.*

In *Eight Weeks to Optimum Health* Dr. Andrew Weil describes sweating as one of the most important mechanisms in natural healing because it allows the body to cleanse itself of unwanted toxins and wastes. It also helps to take the workload off the liver and kidneys, which are chiefly responsible for the detoxification and purification of the blood.

ABOVE Having a regular session in a steam room or sauna is a great means to detoxify. It is a non-strenuous way of creating heat inside the body to dissolve accumulated toxins and help to move them out of the body.

RIGHT Exercise is good for us because it increases the strength of the heart and lungs, develops stamina and muscle tone, improves digestion, and makes skin healthier. It also increases physical endurance, especially through improved breathing, which helps to develop our personal energy levels.

RELAXATION

Today it is easy to find excitement but much more challenging to find tranquillity, relaxation, and peace of mind. Relaxation can help us to eliminate stress and tension from our mind and body, and it is essential for us to remain healthy. If stress and tension are not dealt with, the body can suffer and physical or mental illness can result. For it is only when our immune system is in a relaxed state that it can work effectively to protect us from disease.

The importance of having quiet time for contemplation, and of using relaxation techniques feed the soul and help to cultivate peace of mind, is often overlooked in today's society. Meditation can help us find some inner guidance and wisdom, which is essential for our spiritual health.

Release daily stresses by following some of these simple relaxation practices and techniques.

Learning how to relax

- *If you have a religious belief, evening prayers can help release the day's concerns. Alternatively, a period of quiet contemplation can have the same effect. Daily meditation can also be beneficial – ideally meditate for 10–30 minutes twice a day.*
- *Practise qi gong or yoga. The movements train your mind to relax as well as your body. You gain better control of your breathing, and they can also improve mental performance and emotional stability.*
- *Keep a journal to record and evaluate events in your life. Note down everything for which you feel grateful each day. Then when you are feeling depressed, look at your list.*
- *Schedule quality time with your loved one or family. When you switch off completely from work your mind will relax and let go of all its anxieties and worries.*

- *Have a special place, just for you, to read or to do whatever relaxing hobby appeals.*
- *Have a weekly massage or some other kind of complementary therapy such as shiatsu (pressure point massage) or reiki (hands-on healing) to help you de-stress. View it as an important de-stressor rather than a luxury.*
- *Find a sports center with a flotation tank. Floating in a tank, cut off from the world, deprives your brain of all sensory stimulation and is deeply relaxing.*
- *Use self-hypnosis tapes to calm and relax.*
- *Use self-massage to release tension from your body very quickly. Tap your fingers on your head, shoulders, and down your arms and legs.*

Be more relaxed about life

- *Laugh more – it really is a very positive medicine. It causes muscles to vibrate in places deep inside you that you otherwise would not reach. It is also infectious, so you will encourage other people to feel happy.*
- *Anxieties and negative thoughts prevent relaxation, so try to process them and present a more positive approach to life.*
- *Listen to some relaxing music; it is a potent healing force that can calm the soul. Some pieces of classical music can enable you to relax and learn faster. Use music as an anchor (a tool of recall), and play anything that has happy memories for you.*
- *Practice breathing deeply from the abdomen rather than the upper chest. Sometimes we forget and our breathing gets very shallow, so it is not bringing in enough vital oxygen and we become sluggish and less able to cope.*
- *Look at other ways of controlling the hours you work, maximizing your time so that your free time can be used more effectively.*

BELOW It is important to find ways of letting go of stress. A symptom of stress-overload is having a short fuse and erupting into a rage. Research at the University of North Carolina has shown that if you do this regularly, you are twice as likely to have a heart attack. Sitting in silence and meditating helps you create an inner calm by breathing slowly and emptying your mind.

RIGHT It is essential to build in time to yourself in order to recover your equilibrium. Children should also be encouraged to relax and given space to wind down.

"Never lose an opportunity of seeing anything that is beautiful; for beauty is God's handwriting – a wayside sacrament."
Ralph Waldo Emmerson

We all have a very intimate connection with nature. For thousands of years, humans have sourced all our food, shelter, clothes and tools from nature, and lived closely aligned to its rhythms. Unfortunately, this has changed dramatically over the last 100 years as we have become more detached and seemingly independent from nature. Living mainly indoors, we have become alienated from the natural cycle of change outside. Now we are the poorer for it, as it is the rhythms of the seasons and natural cycles of day and night that stimulate and prompt our own internal rhythms.

Being in tune with the natural harmony around us helps bring us into balance. And in nature everything is in perfect balance, every living thing that grows has its own unique place in the ecological system. Vegetables can be cultivated in harmony, with different plants being grown together to naturally divert any harmful pests. The earth is a system of interconnected life forms that all support each other.

The changing seasons

Witnessing the seasons and experiencing the changes within the animal and plant kingdoms helps us to reaffirm to ourselves the continuity of life. We are reminded that there are times of the day and year when it is more important to be energetic, to be active and to grow, while at other times withdrawal, solitude, and rest are more appropriate before the next phase of renewal begins. We can change our behavior so that we do not try to work against the flow of

nature and start new projects that require much effort in the less stimulating evening hours or during winter.

The beauty of nature

Nature is the most natural de-stressor. Its smells, sounds, beauty, and vibrant life and textures help to calm the mind; its rhythms guide our routines. We can reconnect with the natural world by going outside more, bringing nature closer to us, and also by bringing more nature inside our artificial world.

The splendor of nature excites every one of our senses, including our sense of wonder. Spiritual nourishment is as important to our overall health as eating good food. Our intuition is reawakened and we are reminded of our place in the universe. We have a deep need within us to believe in something larger than ourselves, and nature is our greatest teacher here. Venturing into the natural world allows us to have a sense of belonging that feeds our soul.

Walking in nature

Going out into the natural world brings you directly into contact with the nutrients that are so life enhancing. Walking on the bare soil or grass reconnects you with the essential magnetic energy of the earth, being out in daylight exposes you to the energizing rays of the sun, and being out in the countryside allows you to fill your lungs and breathe in air more deeply.

Create a garden

Bring nature closer to your home by making a garden, a small ecosystem of plant, animal, and bird life that can become a small microcosm of the planet. Use your garden to grow your own organic vegetables. A small patio can provide all

ABOVE Bringing water indoors is a great way to relax a space. The sound of water trickling from a fountain or bubbling over stones can often mask the more intrusive sounds of machinery or the hum of traffic. Water is cooling and refreshing, it stimulates the energy of a room, and it reduces the positively charged ions created by electrical equipment.

RIGHT Plants are no longer a luxury in the home; they are a necessity, because of their ability to purify the air. Their leaves absorb many different chemical pollutants that are then transported to the root system and converted to a source of energy for the plant.

inclined to live outside as Mediterranean families naturally do, but if you dress warmly and build a fire, being out in the fresh air and sunlight will be as nourishing as the food you eat.

The natural inside world

You can bring nature into your home in many different ways so that you reconnect with the world outside. Using natural colors in decoration can make a room feel in tune with the outside world. Oatmeals and creams provide a neutral background tone to which can be added spring greens, summer pinks, and autumnal golds (see pages 112–126).

Flowers bring in good energy, and are another way of bringing color into a room and making it really come alive. Natural materials such as woven baskets, pinecones, driftwood, stones, and logs all link you with the world outside. Use them as ornaments, and change them seasonally to connect you with the passing of time. Make a nature table where you bring in the fruits of the seasons, celebrating the true bounty of nature.

Water is both life-enhancing and energizing, and you can introduce it into your home in several different imaginative ways. Acquire a fish tank, a small fountain built into the wall, or a small water feature (with a pump to recycle the water). Moving water helps to ionize the atmosphere, increasing the number of negative ions in the air and making it a more relaxing environment. Positive ions are created by electrical equipment (among other things), and these can create more stress for the home's occupants. The sound of water is also soothing and can help to mask other noises that may be unpleasant and irritating, such as background traffic.

the fresh herbs in tubs that your kitchen needs; a rooftop area can be converted into a small paradise with lush vegetation and visiting bird life to make you feel more grounded. If you have no garden, put plants in your window boxes and take pleasure in seeing things grow. The variety

of herbs, evergreen, or scented flowering plants that are useful, beautiful, and can be grown in a window box is surprising.

Create an indoor garden, or screen off your patio area so that you can eat outside whatever the weather. People in colder climates are less

Plants are very effective in helping to calm you and reduce stress in the home. They cleanse the air and also ensure that we are not the only living things in an indoor, artificial space. In the 1970s, research was started at NASA to find a way to support life on the moon by treating and recycling air in closed ecological life-support systems. They discovered that plants have an amazing ability to purify and revitalize air. So while also aesthetically pleasing, they actually sustain life in artificial environments, particularly if these are well-sealed for heat conservation and lack natural ventilation.

Dr. Wolverton (part of the NASA team) has tested 50 indoor plants for their ability to neutralize different emissions in the air, and for their ease of growth and maintenance. The highest scoring plants are ranked as follows: Areca Palm, Lady Palm, Bamboo Palm, Rubber Plant, Dracaena, English Ivy, Dwarf Date Palm, Ficus Alii, Boston Fern, Peace Lily, Corn Plant, Golden Pothos, Florist's Mum, Gerbera Daisy and Spider Plants all have high ratings for removing formaldehyde emissions (see pages 33–35).

Aromatic oils distilled from plants can be used as healing remedies and for changing the mood of a room. These essential oils are extracted from the seeds, bark, stems, roots, leaves, and flowers of hundreds of plants. They are effective because our sense of smell is powerful and linked directly to the limbic system of the brain, which controls our moods.

After using these oils you can feel an almost immediate emotional response. Add drops of oil to perfume bowls of dried petals or flowers; put in an oil burner to scent a room; or add a few drops to an atomizer filled with water and spray it around a room.

Stimulating oils that will perk you up include basil, jasmine, peppermint, rosemary, and ylang ylang; relaxing oils to calm you and lower your stress levels include lemon balm, lemon, valerian, sandalwood, bergamot, and lavender; and those which strengthen your nervous system include juniper, clary sage, lavender, and camomile. Find out about how different essential oils can suit different situations and help balance different biological processes.

Earth crystals have very powerful properties, so it helps to understand a bit about them before you fill your home with them. Use a chunk of amethyst for protection around your computer (if you have a pendulum, dowse and ask how effective this is for you), and rose quartz and selenite for harmonizing any geopathic stress. Fresh air will revitalize us, bringing new oxygen in. Always open windows and clear stagnant energy from all your rooms each morning. Natural light is essential to health so sit in sunlight as often as you can, protecting yourself with sunscreen, especially from the harsher rays of midday and hotter climates.

Seasonal ceremonies remind us that the elements of nature have always played a huge part in our lives. As the seasons move from one to the other, each one affects us differently. Observing the ceremonies that whole communities celebrate, such as Harvest time, Thanksgiving, and Christmas, can connect us all globally. A church service or a family meal are the most obvious ways to take part, but there are also hundreds of festivals, such as the Celtic seasonal festivals, celebrated in the past that can be observed today. Rituals can be as simple as lighting candles and displaying floral decorations, but they can be made personal to you, creating great opportunities for family fun and creativity.

RIGHT You don't have to have access to the ground floor to create a garden – they can be anywhere. Be creative and bring in pots and troughs, and develop your own natural haven in the heart of the city. Rooftop vegetation is also very good at helping to improve air quality, especially in areas of traffic pollution.

LEFT AND ABOVE Many people, especially city dwellers, have forgotten what happens at different times of year, because their concerns are so centered on the indoor environment. Bringing elements of nature inside the home helps us to reconnect with the rhythms of life. Keep an eye out for stones, feathers, shells, twigs, and cones when you are out walking. Placing them on a windowsill or creating a nature table will increase your sense of the sacred in your home. Keep renewing it as the seasons change throughout the year.

The earth is a huge magnet. It has a massive magnetic field emanating from it, and it is this powerful unseen radiation of energy from the earth that is essential to life on the planet.

The advantages of magnetism

We cannot exist without good earth energies, and our well-being and vitality depend on the amount of energy we can produce. It is now believed that only 70 percent of the energy we need can be generated by a good diet including the right vitamins and minerals. The other 30 percent comes from magnetism, and it is this non nutritional energy that enables our cells to work efficiently. Magnetism enables us to cope with the constant environmental damage that we are suffering from chemicals and man-made electromagnetic fields. It also helps to maintain a good supply of oxygen for cells, and maintains the right alkaline pH balance.

Every night as we sleep with our bodies lying flat close to the earth, each of our tired cells receives a boost similar to that from a battery charger. The sleep process is designed to restore our immune systems. Our brain acts as a control center organizing the important repairs that the body needs. But if our brain has distracting interference from other electromagnetic fields, such as those emanating from clock radios, and is not able to communicate properly with the rest of the body, we suffer. These other fields also affect our connection to the earth's helpful magnetic field.

Unfortunately, we are now experiencing lower levels of supportive magnetic energy than our ancestors because the earth's field is weakening. There has been a 7 percent loss in strength over the last 100 years alone (according to George J. Washnis, author of *Discovery of*

Magnetic Health). We also now live in modern urban environments where many homes are constructed from concrete and steel, which act as a barrier to the complex and subtle magnetic energies that are naturally absorbed through the earth.

Today we are constantly assaulted by harmful electromagnetic vibrations. They cannot be seen, but are largely generated by our quest to modernize our lifestyle. The proliferation of state-of-the-art personal communications and television and radio signals means that our bodies have not yet adjusted to all these different radiations.

Artificial electromagnetic waves

Before the 1920s when radio transmissions started, people had never experienced the force of artificially created electromagnetic waves on earth. Evidence presented by George Washnis is now increasingly suggesting that these artificial distortions adversely affect the delicate chemical and electrical balance of our immune systems, causing much of our stress, and contributing to cancers and a host of other bodily disorders.

Natural cures

For thousands of years, ancient civilizations recognized the power of magnetism not only to balance the body, but to heal it as well. Modern medicine has followed the route of pharmacology, with drugs being the first choice to heal different illnesses. However, there is growing evidence that shows that bio-electromagnetic medicine, which includes magnetotherapy, could solve many of the conditions not cured by drugs. Dr. William H. Philpott is a doctor who has successfully used magnetotherapy for thousands

of patients. He was quoted in *Discovering of Magnetic Health* as saying that magnetism boosts human energy levels, supports the proper functioning of the immune system, and, in raising alkaline pH levels of bodily fluids, can kill cancer cells.

Magnetism has long been a favored healing modality in Japan, but it was not until the space programs started in the 1950s that Western

ABOVE AND RIGHT Being in contact with the earth's magnetic field supports our well-being and vitality. Unfortunately, in modern times less of this beneficial radiation is getting through to us because of the interference caused by human-generated electromagnetic fields, leading to poorer health.

countries began to recognize the value and potential of magnetism. The early astronauts returned to earth in physical distress, unable to walk and with loss of bone density. Investigations by NASA showed that this was caused by the astronauts being taken out of the influence of the earth's magnetic field. As soon as the resonance was simulated inside the space capsule, no further health problems were suffered. George Washnis says that an increasing number of researchers now recognize that the way to correct the stress symptoms caused by a deficiency in magnetism is to provide consistent exposure to artificial sources.

Several companies now manufacture products that allow people to reconnect with this essential energy of the earth. Low-gauss magnets in mattresses enable people to benefit fully from the earth's energy while they sleep, rather than the weak resonance that is normally emitted because of disturbances from EM pollution and modern building materials. Seat covers incorporating magnets support people sitting in the high electromagnetic field that emanates from their cars and computers. Innovative magnetic insoles that people wear in shoes keep people in contact with the earth's energy all day, even though they are normally indoors in man-made environments.

Magnetic therapy is a treatment using this therapeutic energy. It is simple, non-invasive, has virtually no risks, and has a success rate of 70–90 percent according to the numerous studies quoted by George Washnis.

How magnetism works

Nobody really knows how it works, but hundreds of double-blind studies around the world have proved its efficacy. It seems to raise the pH levels in the body and provide a more alkaline environment for cell survival. Cancer cells prefer an acidic environment and cannot survive in an alkaline one. Many of the foods we eat and the stressful way we conduct our lives causes acidity to build up. In particular, our diets have become much more acidic over the last 40 years (see pages 74–77).

Cell activity also seems to be boosted by magnetism. Each cell has an electromagnetic charge, and by applying a magnetic field, you can stimulate the cell's ability to flush out toxins and absorb more nutrients. Broken bones have been found to heal four times more quickly in a magnetic field.

The Japanese are great advocates of magnetotherapy; 30 million of them use magnetic products, and 10 percent of the population sit or sleep on magnetic pads. There has to be a valuable lesson to be learnt here since the World Health Organization has identified Japan as the healthiest country in the world. In comparison, the US spends $2 trillion annually on healthcare, and yet the WHO only lists us as the 24th healthiest country in the world.

How to use magnetism

- *Walk on the earth barefoot. This can bring you directly in contact with the earth's magnetic field.*
- *Use products that bring the earth's energy into your home, such as magnetic seats and mattress pads, on a daily basis.*
- *Investigate the various magnetic health products that can act as an aid to rebalancing the body and general well-being.*
- *Drink magnetized water by placing a glass on a magnet for an hour. Use magnetic laundry balls, which change the molecular structure of water in the same way as chemical detergents.*

THE SUN

All life forms depend upon sunlight, and for millions of years it has nourished us daily. It helps control most of our bodily functions, especially our de-stressing mechanisms, and keeps our inner body clock aligned to the earth's natural daily rhythms.

The sun's powerful rays

We need the full spectrum of the sun's radiation for our health, and that includes the infrared waves providing heat, the ultraviolet (UV) wavelengths, and of course the visible light, which contains all the colors of the rainbow.

UV light

UV light stimulates blood circulation, lowers blood pressure, increases the metabolism of protein, lessens fatigue, stimulates the production of white blood cells (part of our defense system), helps create endorphins (the "happy" hormones), and assists the assimilation of calcium and the production of vitamin D for healthy bones. Because UV light is so important to us, Dr. John Ott recommends that we spend six hours a day in daylight, whether by an indoor window or by going outside. Bear in mind that most people now spend almost 90 percent of their time indoors, so we really need to make an effort to be in daylight.

Full spectrum light bulbs (see page 60) are the only form of artificial light that contain the health-giving UV rays. We take in the goodness from light through our skin and also through our eyes, so it is important not to always wear sunglasses in natural sunlight.

Architect Christopher Day says that inadequate light causes hormonal changes which in humans is called SAD (Seasonal Affective Disorder) and is responsible for the total infertility of indoor-housed sheep. This leads to the speculation that daylight has a bearing on human fertility.

The importance of natural light was also discussed on pages 55–56, so in this section we want to look further at the role infrared waves, particularly far infrared, play in keeping us in good health.

Far infrared waves

Within the natural spectrum of electromagnetic waves generated from the sun are infrared waves. Of these, the far infrared waves (FIR) have a natural resonance with water and all living organisms on the planet. Humans can absorb FIR waves easily; they penetrate deep into our bodies creating a uniform warmth unlike the uneven, intense heat from near infrared waves generated from electric bar fires and ovens. It is this comforting warmth that we give out when we embrace someone or cradle a baby.

FIR waves are especially good at agitating the water molecules in our bodies, enabling them to release stored toxins. It is these hidden toxins that not only contribute to degenerative illness, but experts now believe are responsible for aging. FIR waves vibrate at a frequency similar to that of the human body, and so are able to penetrate deep within it. This means that they can support the micro-circulatory system reactivating and revitalizing cells and organs. Consequently wastes are removed more effectively, and the metabolic rate (an indicator of good health) is increased.

The overall effects of this strengthen the immune system and make a person feel more energetic and full of vitality. If there were some way that we could utilize the FIR radiation from our bodies, then we could not only keep ourselves warm, but also speed up our detoxification. This would mean that we could keep more balanced healthwise, and some experts believe that the aging process could be slowed down.

Utilizing FIR warmth

A range of products manufactured in the Far East is utilizing materials with bio-ceramic fibers that can reflect back the FIR warmth that our bodies give out. Currently available are items such as health and sports bandages for joints. There are also bedding products that allow you to be bathed in beneficial and detoxifying FIR waves while you are asleep.

FIR is also good at lowering acidity levels that create the environments preferred by disease and mutant cells. More recently, FIR materials are starting to be used in clothes, so that people can wear items that can make a significant contribution to their health.

Although not so readily available yet, the technology also exists to use FIR-reflecting material around the home, in wall paints, saunas, hair dryer and ovens.

FAR LEFT Sunlight is nourishment. Many people in the developed world now spend 90 percent of their time indoors and miss out on the essential wavelengths that support functions, such as the production of hormones that stimulate positive moods. In addition, the sun is a source of inspiration, as its energy awakens and motivates us.

Everything that exists around us consists of vibrating energy, including our homes. While we can revitalize our homes by redecorating or cleaning out physical dust and debris that collect over time, there are occasions when further work is needed to shift the energy of our homes. Psychic cleaning, space clearing, or home harmonizing are all ways to help us make our homes feel better. You can learn some simple methods to improve your home's atmosphere.

If you have ever walked into a room where there has been an argument you may recall feeling that you could have "cut the atmosphere with a knife". You cannot see anything, but you can sense what has taken place as there is a definite uncomfortable feeling about the space. You may recall the difference that you can feel before and after a thunderstorm. The distinct tension in the air only starts to lift when the electrical storm begins and the cleansing rain

comes. It is this kind of unease that we can experience in the atmosphere or energy of our own homes. If this is not properly dealt with, it can start to drain our own energy levels, eroding our physical and emotional well-being.

There are some simple techniques you can use that change the ambience of your home and uplift its energy by changing the vibrations.

How cleansing can help

Cleansing rituals help to raise the quality of the atmosphere in the home in a very subtle way. It is possible to experience a wonderful lightness afterwards, as if someone has made all the lights brighter. It gives the house a spiritual vitality that you will find very energizing and uplifting.

When you want to make changes in your life or are hoping that something specific will happen, a cleansing and harmonizing ceremony will certainly help. It enables you to change the

vibrations that are hindering you, and allows you to have a clearer space in which to set your intentions. The techniques are very useful if you feel tired and stuck, and seem unable to move forward in life, as though something invisible is weighing you down and holding you back.

The next pages outline the simple techniques that you can use to harmonize your home yourself. However, you can also choose to call in professional clearers who are experienced in the psychic clearing of houses and have the expertise to work with energy at a deeper level, perhaps creating bigger shifts where they are needed (see www.thehealthyhome.com). You can harmonize your own home as often as you like, and you can also create simple ceremonies that just tweak the energy on a weekly basis, keeping your home fresh and energetic.

Remember, energy flowing easily and freely through your home, your body, and your life, is the basis of good health and well-being.

When to harmonize your home

- *Whenever you want to make a fresh start and boost the overall energy.*
- *When moving from an old home and when settling into a new one.*
- *When you are trying to sell your property and want to attract a buyer.*
- *To improve your luck, attract more money into your life, or draw in a new relationship.*
- *To cleanse any space where you feel you want to clear out other people's negative energies, maybe after someone has visited, or even when you are staying in a hotel room.*
- *Have a ceremony after somebody has been ill for a while, or if there has been a death in the family.*
- *When you cannot get yourself motivated to move forward, or just to cheer yourself up.*

RIGHT Lighting incense is a very quick and simple way of shifting energy in a room. Use it as an alternative to chemical air fresheners. Experiment with different fragrances for different moods.

FAR RIGHT Although the previous occupants may have left, a trace of their energy will remain. Harmonizing a new home will mean that the period of time for you to adjust to it will be that much shorter.

Preparation for home harmonizing

Before you start, be clear about what you want to happen or create. Why do you feel it is necessary to change the atmosphere of your home? Perhaps it is a new property, or an old one and you want to clear out the energies of the previous occupants. Maybe you have been ill, out of work, or have had a lot of arguments in your relationship, and you want to cleanse and raise the energy levels.

Then get in touch with your home. Relax completely, perhaps using meditation, and ask permission from your home to activate this process. Try to do this the night before and visualize the outcome you want to achieve. Then prepare yourself mentally by being calm, "grounded" (down to earth), and focused on

what you are about to do. Work in silence, and remove any jewelry and your shoes to avoid distraction and help to develop your intuitive senses. Sensitize your hands by rubbing them together and then holding an imaginary grapefruit. Expand this slowly to a small melon and you should feel a ball of energy in your cupped hands.

Clean and tidy your home, clearing out as much clutter as you can. (You can do a quick house cleansing without this, but in order to create a real shift in the energy you really do need the physical clearing first.) When all the nooks and crannies have been dusted and wiped, and all floors have been vacuumed or swept, you will notice a big difference in the overall atmosphere. Every sack of clutter taken out will lift the energy. Also turn off all equipment that makes a noise. Finally, open some windows to help shift the negative energies you want to clear out.

Simple steps for house cleansing

1 *Set up your equipment. Buy some flowers (to brighten the atmosphere) and candles, smudge sticks or incense, sea or rock salt, lavender or geranium aromatherapy oils, and find a bell and other instruments to make sounds like a drum. Arrange all these on a special table (an altar covered with a beautiful cloth) that will be the focus of your work.*

2 *Dislodge any stagnant energy with sound. Start at the door, then use your hands to clap around the edges and corners of each room, or use a drum to beat out the vibrations, which have become stagnant. If any areas feel heavy, clap or drum louder. Keep focused and have fun.*

3 *Purify a room's energy using the Air element with smoke or incense. Light a sage smudge stick,*

blow it out, and hold above a fireproof dish to catch any sparks. Waft the perfumed herbal smoke in a clockwise direction around each room with a feather or your hand. Alternatively, blow smoke from a smoldering incense stick around the corners of the room.

4 *You can use the sacred vibration of sound by ringing bells around the edges of each room. You can also bring in the Water element, by misting a room with water perfumed with a few drops of cleansing aromatherapy oils such as rosemary or lavender. Keep affirming throughout your cleansing process: "this home will bless everyone who lives here," or whatever seems appropriate to help to refresh your house. Keep in mind your intention or your desires.*

5 *Light candles in the rooms to bring in the powerful energy of the Fire element. Salt represents the Earth element, and can be placed in tiny dishes on the floor in the four corners of the house (leave for 24 hours).*

6 *Close your ceremony by sitting quietly, thanking the house, and blessing it for your future. Let the candles burn down but extinguish them if you have to leave. Tap out the smoldering edges of the smudge stick and save for another ceremony.*

For details of trained practitioners who can evaluate the energy of your home and perform the ceremony with you, look on the website www.thehealthyhome.com.

Color is something we experience throughout our lives, every waking day, whether we are indoors or outdoors. It comes to us in the spectrum of light from the sun as electromagnetic energy. Within this spectrum is a rainbow of colors, each one projecting a different vibration.

Although we see color with our eyes, color energy is also absorbed through our skin and the energy field around our bodies (our aura). It not only affects us psychologically but also physiologically, as experiments have shown that blind people will also react to color.

Color affects our body, mind, and emotions, and often we have favorite colors that we like to wear and use in our homes. Color psychology as a science is commonly used in product packaging and retail environments, yet we could all make a huge difference to our lives if we applied the knowledge more at home.

Color is the one key area over which we have the most control when we are designing our living spaces. The more we try to understand it and explore how it influences our moods, emotions, health, and performance, the more it will improve our lives. Think about how you want to feel in a room, and see what qualities are within you that you would like to bring out by the use of color.

The energy of color

When you understand more about the vibrational energy of color, you can easily change how a room feels so that it supports whatever mood or purpose you need. It also gives you greater flexibility because it means you can change the room's atmosphere very quickly by repainting the walls, rather than having to replace a carpet or curtains. For example, you can make a room much more cozy and more relaxing by visually bringing down a high ceiling by using a dark shade of paint.

As all color influences our thoughts and behavior, it is important to pay attention to the color of clothes that you wear, and the colors that you surround yourself with at home and at work. Any color that dominates can have a profound effect.

How color affects the body

When colored light enters the body it affects the major gland of the endocrine system – the pituitary – which controls the hormones released by the endocrine glands. These regulate many bodily functions, including energy levels, metabolism, appetite, sexual drive, growth, and sleep. Exposure to red light, for example, stimulates the heart and circulation and also releases adrenaline, which stimulates appetite and creativity. Surround yourself with reds, and you will never relax. Yellow stimulates the brainwaves and can make you feel mentally alert and positive; blue relates to the throat and thyroid glands, and is a color that soothes and calms.

Color can be used to bring about physical, mental, and emotional balance. Blues are at the cooler end of the color spectrum and are more calming, while reds are at the warmer end and are more stimulating. These affect our mind and emotions subliminally, but there are also colors with which we have a natural affinity because they resonate with our own inner vibrations. When choosing interior colors for your home, it is important that they feel right for you. Also remember that our choice of colors, both in terms of our clothes and our home, very powerfully communicates just what we are about and how we feel.

How to use different colors

Choosing the colors to decorate your home is very personal. To find out the colors that you like the most, look at a paint color chart or color wheel and note the ones that seem most appealing. Remember that shades of the same color affect a room in differing ways.

Combining colors

A harmonious color scheme in the home needs to include both warm and cool shades. Colors next to each other on the color wheel, and those opposite will combine well:

- Red goes well with orange and purple and complements green
- Orange goes well with red and yellow and complements blue
- Yellow goes well with orange and green and complements purple
- Green goes well with yellow and blue and complements red
- Blue goes well with green and purple and complements orange
- Purple goes well with red and blue and complements yellow

RIGHT The green in this hall creates a calming space for visitors to arrive in, while the colored glass adds an upbeat lively feeling.

FAR RIGHT The orange in this other hallway is also welcoming and indicates a sociable host. These bright colors will enhance the experience of anybody arriving here.

Key words for color

Purple/Violet – regal, noble, artistic, intuitive, meditative, mystical, spiritual.

Red – warming, stimulates activity, puts people on alert, romantic love, passion, vigor, full of life, aggression, impatience, opulence.

Pink – nurturing, calming, maternal feelings.

Orange – joy, courage, happiness, good digestion, conversation.

Yellow – focus, mental alertness, uplifting, vitality, reduces tension.

Green – healing, harmony, love, abundance, growth, money, balance.

Blue – coolness, calm, peace, sleep-inducing, reflection, inspiration.

Brown – earthiness, grounding, stable.

White – purity, innocence, openness, magic, cleanliness.

Black – death, negativity, power, mystery, strength, magic, depth, depression.

Purple

Purple is a distinctively aristocratic and royal color. It is not generally a popular primary color in homes. However, it also has spiritual associations, so if you want to develop your psychic abilities and need a room or area for meditation, a shade of purple on the walls will be able to provide just the right vibrations. It is a heavy color, and should be used sparingly. Exposing too much purple can cause depression. Used with splashes of gold, it can give a regal touch to the furnishings of an elegant living room. A more mauve color can create a mystical atmosphere in a home.

Pink

Pink is a shade of red with a fair bit of white added, but instead of being energizing it is very soothing and reassuring. Tests carried out at the US Naval Correctional Center in Seattle (1978) with hostile youths, showed that when they were placed in a room that was painted pink they became calm after·15 minutes and this behaviour continued for 30 minutes after leaving the room. Pink color waves make glands release hormones that restrict the release of adrenaline, which in turn slows down the heart muscle, making it more difficult to react quickly to stress or aggression. Pinks promote

gentleness and are associated with maternal, nurturing love as opposed to romantic love. It would be a very supportive color in the bedroom of a divorced person.

ABOVE Where pink is the dominant color, a room will always have a gentle and loving feel to it.

RIGHT The use of gold here with purple makes it a bold and dramatic room, as well as a retreat in which to reflect.

Red

Red is a warm, stimulating color that increases blood pressure, the beat of the heart, the rate of respiration, brain activity, and the biorhythms of the body. This color does cause people to become more agitated, so time appears to pass more slowly in a red room. It is a very physical shade, the color of fire and blood, symbols of power, drive, and life force.

This color is very passionate one. As red is known to increase the production of adrenaline, there needs to be some check on its use or excitement can quickly turn into aggression.

Red is also associated with courage, positive attitude, and burning desire. Be careful how you use it in your home. A touch of red is more effective than painting a whole red wall as some would find that too strong to live with. We all react differently to color, so a quiet introverted person may be thrown off balance by the use of red, while another could thrive on its stimulation. When used in color therapy, red is particularly helpful for the easing of stiff muscles and joints, and it will help to boost a sluggish circulation.

Red, orange, and yellow have been found to irritate people more than blue, green, and violet.

ABOVE Red accessories energize this room, livening up the other pale colors, boosting flagging vitality.

RIGHT The dark pink and red walls in this hallway create an impressive and dramatic space – much easier to move through than to spend time in.

Blue

Blue is a cool color which has the opposite effect of red. Exposure to blue can release eleven different tranquilizing hormones in the body. It can calm us when we get stressed, but if you use too much you will never get motivated. Time seems to pass more quickly in a blue or green room since we feel more relaxed. Some people may even get the blues by being in an environment with too much of the color.

Blue promotes passivity and is extremely conducive to sleep. Research has shown that placebo tablets colored blue are more likely to sedate people than pink ones. This can make it a good color for the bedroom of an insomniac but it may be too cold as a general bedroom color for most people.

Since color affects our perception of temperature, we can feel warmer in a red room and cooler in a blue one. Color preferences change with the seasons, so people tend to prefer cooling blues in high temperatures to make them feel more comfortable. Paint a hot sunny conservatory blue and it will feel cooler.

Blue is associated with water, contemplation, communication, and intelligence – it is a peaceful and reflective colour. If you want to bring any of these qualities to a room then introduce shades of blue with flowers, lampshades, artwork, and throws.

Color affects children too – bright, active tones will support and stimulate them in play areas. Babies will look longer at brighter colors, so these are not suitable when you want the children to settle down and sleep. The tranquilizing qualities in blue make it ideal to use around children's sleeping areas, either on the walls or in the bedding, since the effect of the color does not depend on it being seen.

Color tips

- *Strong colors can visually reduce a room size, so if you want the feeling of more space, choose paler shades.*
- *Keep background colors monochromatic and neutral, and let the color come from accessories, paintings, and furnishings. Bright colors have more effect against a neutral background.*
- *Rooms with little natural light need pale colors to emphasize what is there. Sunlight is an important constituent because it contains all the colors in the spectrum. Light colors will reflect more sunlight.*
- *Dark colors reflect less light, so choose them for a room that is used for night-time dining or relaxation, and illuminate the interior with soft lights and lamps.*

RIGHT This room would be ideal for a city dweller, because both the color and the real leaf wall decoration provide a restorative setting and a strong connection to the natural world. Green is a good antidote to work fatigue.

LEFT The striking blue used on this wall creates a cool, calm environment in the hallway. The lighter blue tone promotes efficiency and order, which helps to keep the space clear and uncluttered.

Green

Green is the color of balance, which is at the center of the rainbow. It creates harmony, stability, and healing, and is also associated with clarity, understanding, and issues of the heart, particularly selfless and unconditional love. It is the color of nature and can be used therapeutically in the home to give a feeling of open space. Greenery is also important to have in the home since it helps us connect with the natural world outside. The calming effect of green helps us tolerate a noisy environment. It is traditional for television studios and theaters to have a "green room" where artistes can relax before a performance, as the vibration of green helps to quell nervousness.

Eating green foods encourages detoxification of the body and enhances physical stamina. Green is also an important aid in physical healing and for rebalancing the psyche in mental illness. A green environment will boost fatigue, alleviate shock, and provide a tonic for the whole body. It is a reassuring and safe color to choose for any room in the house. It is the most balancing of all the colors, and even when not used for the decorating scheme or furnishings it can be introduced simply with plants.

Green is also associated with growth and money; it is a good color to introduce into a working environment, but it needs to be combined with other colors so that people do not become too laid-back and relaxed.

Orange

Orange is the color of action and optimism. It is joyful, warm-hearted, and tolerant, and is associated with good humor and friendship. People who favor wearing orange enjoy being the life and soul of the party. It is a color that helps break down barriers and stimulates energy in a more subtle way than red. It gives people strength to cope with adversity.

Warm orange tones can be ideal as a color scheme in a dining room to enhance the pleasure of social dinners, since they help to stimulate conversation and aid digestion. The effects of red, on the other hand, can be just too strong, particularly for everyday dining.

Each color has distinct physiological influences on the body, with blue and red having the most marked effect. Orange promotes cheerfulness and will boost the motivation levels of people coming to work if used for a staff entrance. Place a round dish of oranges at the center of a group and watch how the discussion becomes more animated, but not aggressive as it can do with red.

Color therapy practitioners use colors to heal. They would recommend wearing orange underwear that covers your stomach area if your digestion is slow or difficult.

LEFT People feel good when bathed in sunlight or the color that represents it. As it also fosters mental clarity, this color would make a good background in a room where someone had to work from home and wanted to stay cheerful and motivated.

Yellow

Yellow is an intellectual color representing wisdom and enlightenment. If you want to stimulate your thinking abilities and write or speak with greater clarity, then wear yellow clothing and introduce some yellow flowers into your home, or use yellow in a study.

It is a color that helps to focus attention and foster new ideas. Yellow is most closely associated with sunlight – hopeful, joyful, and uplifting. It is a great color to combine with other colors or to be used as a contrast. In terms of using color as therapy, yellow can have a great impact on our mental balance and, in turn, our physical well-being. It quickens our reflexes and reduces hesitation, something very important to the men and women who go to work as fire fighters while wearing their bright yellow waterproof coats.

Yellow makes people feel good, especially when most of us spend 90 percent of our time indoors. Using yellow in rooms boosts self-confidence, promotes good-natured feelings, and reduces the likelihood of any upsets.

A room with yellow and sunflowers in its decor would alleviate feelings of depression. Shades of yellow should be chosen carefully for furniture and walls, and can be over-stimulating for some bedrooms. Use yellow wherever you want to bring the energy of sunshine to a situation or corner. It helps to get rid of toxins in the body and reduces any negative thinking.

ABOVE LEFT Bright, cheerful orange used in the kitchen denotes a happy, confident home and is always welcoming to guests.

ABOVE RIGHT Orange encourages movement, so it is a particularly effective color when used in a hall.

Brown

Brown symbolizes the color of earth and can be a good shade for making people feel protected and grounded. A brown carpet can be used in a room over a garage, or in a high-level apartment to help people feel more connected to the earth.

There are numerous different shades of brown, and those with more reddish hues have more warmth and vibrancy. It is important not to choose one that is too dark and murky, as this will have a negative effect.

Using brown can make a home or newly decorated room appear much more established, as it is connected with roots and depth. It brings a sense of security and a feeling of time passing. However, large areas of brown can feel very heavy and may lead people to become introverted or to feel depressed.

Of the seasons, brown is most closely connected with autumn when the leaves fall, and a cycle of nature comes to an end ready for a new one to begin. Shades of autumn can bring glorious brown hues, ranging from tan to coffee.

Brown is not a primary color from the rainbow, and most shades are not reflective. They absorb light, but the red tones within the color will mostly offer warmth and reassuring comfort, although they lack the vitality of red itself. It is a color that should be used with great care, and, sparingly at that.

Brown has associations with "holding on" which can be unhealthy, especially if relating to the past. However, it is a very grounding color and can be useful in a room where you want to reinforce a sense of connection.

Beige and oatmeal

Beige and oatmeal are neutral colors that generally denote a feeling of winter. When they are used on their own in the home they create an environment which is very cool, so this can be useful when the temperature outside is hot.

However, if the local environment is cold then these shades may seem chilling and uncomfortable unless they are warmed up by mixing with other shades. Some factories use beige and light blue to encourage tidiness.

The use of the colors light cream and oatmeal are becoming more and more popular, particularly because they sit so well with natural materials such as wood, cane, wicker, stone, and wood. Beige is always easy on the eye, very comfortable to live with, and an ideal choice for creating a minimalist space or a room that is a gentle, calming background to a stressful life.

LEFT Using brown in a newly created or decorated room can make it feel like it has already existed for a long time. This room has a reassuring feel to it and could increase a person's sense of stability. If using a lot of dark brown you must also have natural light to balance it.

RIGHT The colors in this interior provide a tranquil setting where the senses do not feel bombarded.

White

White is a non-color that blends all the colors of the rainbow and will reflect natural light. It is the color of purity in most cultures and offers protection, like the white flag of a peace negotiator. As a wall color it can create a very stark environment, although it can make a room look larger and the ceilings appear higher.

White can work well if the color is used simply as a neutral backdrop for brighter colors chosen for furnishings, accessories, or pictures. This combination will make the harsh effect of white recede. Its plainness can be warmed up by making it beige or off-white. White on its own can be unfriendly and sterile, but it can increase our sense of space as we spend so much time indoors. Use it as the base color, then bring in other colors.

You can change the feeling of a room seasonally by decorating white or pale rooms with colored tapestries, wall hangings, cushions, drapes, and pictures that reflect the colors of the cycles of nature. Introduce lively yellows and greens in the spring, bright pink/terracottas and cooling blues in the summer, earthy tones in the autumn, and warm reds in the winter to raise the temperature.

Black

Black is not a true color. It is largely associated with death and funerals and has negative connotations in most cultures, but it also indicates mystery and the unknown. The darkness of the color can feel very frightening, or it can signal an inner journey of discovery. Black is effective when used as an accent color in a brighter decorating scheme, but too much of it can make a room look smaller, and induce a lack of hope and depression.

Today, many people are out of balance emotionally and unsure of how to project their true feelings. This may be the reason for the increase in use of black as the primary color for clothes used by people in urban environments. It has become a sort of uniform, and indicates a disconnection from our true selves.

ABOVE White in a bedroom creates a calm atmosphere. Bring in a warm yellow so that it won't feel so cold.

RIGHT A single color, especially a bold one such as black, can have a dominating and profound effect in a space. A background of white will visually intensify any other color that you use.

THREE

Healthy Rooms

In this section we bring together many of the principles already discussed to give you some practical reminders and tips for creating healthy environments. This is not so much about how spaces are rearranged as about an attitude of mind, which will influence the choices you make about what to bring into your home. Many of the topics we have discussed that have the greatest influence on us are invisible and hardly ever considered by the average householder.

THE LIVING ROOM: A PLACE FOR SOCIABLE RELAXATION

The living room is an important gathering place in the home, so all family members should feel that it is pleasing and comfortable. The room should be spacious enough for everyone to be accommodated without feeling cramped. It should have a selection of inviting chairs, as opposed to having one really luxurious seat that is favored and fought over by all. Avoid seating that looks good but in reality is not comfortable for any length of time. A television will draw people into the room because its electrical sounds and artificial activity will naturally attract people's attention – however, there are other methods of bringing people together. Look at ways of creating the right kind of lighting, especially in the evening, so the room feels illuminated but not too bright; a lit fire is a welcoming sight; background music can give atmosphere; and the presence of a pet is homely and relaxing.

KEY

one The white walls and cream and brown tones provide a neutral background, giving a restful, calm quality to the room. The mood could be adapted by replacing the cushions and throws with more vibrant colors such as peach, orange and red.

two Always bring elements of the natural world, such as plants and flowers, into an indoor space. With flowers, keep the water fresh as the stagnant energy from dirty water is extremely unhealthy.

three For the living room the focal point is invariably the fireplace. A real log or coal fire is both therapeutic and good for air circulation, and the heat it generates is healthier than central heating. During seasons when the fireplace is not used, red flowers and plants can be placed in the grate as a centerpiece. Try to avoid using the television as a focal point. Conceal it when not in use.

four Open the curtains or shutters to let the natural daylight flood in, even when you are not using the room, since this helps to stimulate

the room's energy. Aim to sit where there is the most possible daylight as your body benefits from this nourishment.

five Make sure you have a balance of different types of lighting. In addition to a central lighting fixture, smaller and lower lamps are helpful for close work such as reading but also create a more restful ambience.

six When you have a large painting in the room taking a reasonably prominent position, ensure that it

is an image that reflects something you enjoy or an aspect of the life you want to have.

seven The healthiest choice for flooring is a wooden floor covered with wool or cotton rugs. These natural materials are beneficial, especially for people with breathing difficulties and allergies.

eight Candlelight is an easy way to change the mood of a room at the end of the day, giving it a special, softened atmosphere.

LEFT This room has the best flooring possible, particularly if any family members suffer from breathing ailments such as asthma. Natural wooden floors are easily cleaned, and they harbor far less dust than wall-to-wall carpets. For extra comfort you can cover the floor with natural cotton or wool rugs that have not been treated with pesticides. The weeping fig tree in the window has been shown to be one of the top ten houseplants that are good at removing formaldehyde from indoor environments. This harmful chemical is found not only in the particle board used to make furniture, but also in carpet backing, adhesives, and everyday items like face tissues. The tall snake plant by the fireplace is virtually indestructible, making it easy to look after. A pair of plants in your living room is a good beginning, but it is preferable to have more abundant greenery.

ABOVE LEFT Be careful not to store too much in a room where you want to relax. The living room may well be the ideal – if not the only – place to keep your treasured collection of books, but it is important to check the shelves seasonally to see what you can pass onto someone or store elsewhere. This will help to keep the energy of the room moving and prevent it from stagnating. It would be a good idea to use a dark room like this more in the evenings, and to spend the bulk of your time indoors in a brighter room that will allow the natural light to nourish you.

ABOVE This cool, low-stress environment would be particularly supportive for someone with a stressful job. The natural wood and cotton seating and the neutral colors of the floor and walls add to the simplicity of the room. You could introduce more vibrant colors to suit your mood or the season – yellow, for example, will instantly cheer up a space. If you have lighting close to the seating as in this room, it is important not to use low-energy lights, which emit high EMF radiation.

THE KITCHEN: THE HEART OF THE HOME

In her cookbook *The Changing Seasons,* health expert Aveline Kushi says "Our ability to think and act is a reflection of our state of physical and mental health, which has its foundation in the food we cook and eat. To master the art of cooking...is to master the art of life, for the greatness and destiny of all people reflects, and is limited by, the quality of their daily food." The kitchen is not only the heart of the home, it is also the place where we can make the biggest impact on our health through the foods we eat and how we prepare them. The quality of energy around the food will affect it, so the atmosphere in the kitchen needs to be calm, relaxed but sufficiently inspiring to make you want to cook. It does require a certain level of commitment to health to make the effort to plan ahead so that you can prepare fresh ingredients, but a kitchen that is well-lit but not too bright, which is kept tidy and in good order, will always be a welcoming and comfortable environment to cook in.

KEY

one Good lighting is important. Lamps with incandescent bulbs are good, as are fluorescent strip lights, if they are full spectrum. Areas for working with sharp knives will need the brightest illumination.

two A good source of natural light supplements artificial lighting and makes the room bright and welcoming all day long.

three Natural materials such as wooden floors and cupboards, marble surfaces and wicker storage create a relaxing feel, as opposed to high-stress shiny surfaces, gleaming metal, and glossy laminates.

four The central island makes this kitchen more sociable, and allows others to help with food preparation. Avoid the use of sharp edges and corners – here the corners are rounded so it is easier to move around – especially near the stove where the cook will spend most of their time. Store knives in a block or out of sight.

five Keep the kitchen clean and tidy at all times so that it is ready for the preparation of the next meal.

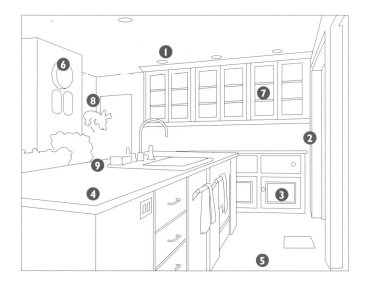

Wooden floors are best; they are comfortable to stand on and easy to keep clean.

six A large, clear clock acts as a strong focal point in the room and is useful for timing the various elements of a meal. Being conscious of the time helps to make sure that mealtimes are regular, which our bodies prefer.

seven Glass doors allow you to see what is stored in each cupboard and have everything to hand. Check cupboards regularly, and throw away things that have gone past their use-by date. Only keep the things that you often need in the kitchen – move "special occasion" crockery elsewhere, if possible.

eight Fresh flowers or plants provide a link with the outside world and bring beauty into a space where you are focusing on health.

nine Use natural alternatives to chemical cleaners whenever possible. It is best to wipe surfaces with hot water and some drops of tea tree oil – a natural disinfectant.

LEFT Having a dining table in your kitchen is advisable since having meals in front of the television is not ideal. If you watch the news while eating, you will absorb the negativity of bad news while you digest your food. Creating a sociable environment for eating, however, will enable you to take full nourishment from your food. I would strongly advise cooking with a gas oven, rather than a microwave or an electric oven. Whatever cooking method you use, turn on the extractor fan when you are cooking to allow any by-products to escape. Blue colors are calm and cool, so this color scheme would provide a supportive setting if yours is a high-stress lifestyle. For others it might not be welcoming enough to motivate them to cook. Check the energy of each color (see pages 112–113) when choosing your scheme.

ABOVE This kitchen feels like the heart of the home, a place where the family can gather. It is a very social room, as people can either sit down and relax or help with the preparations. It is good to have fresh food on display, rather than cupboards full of cans and packets. Bowls of vegetables and fresh fruit and jars of beans and pasta create an atmosphere of abundance, encouraging you to cook fresh food. This room seems warm and welcoming because of the natural light, the curves in the design of the cupboards, chairs and table legs, and the bright red and white flooring. There are additional spotlights above the surfaces to provide good task lighting. Few kitchens have space for more than one trash cans, so try to create a waste-management system in a utility room so you can recycle paper, cans, bottles, and food waste separately to other trash.

THE DINING ROOM: A PLACE TO NOURISH THE FAMILY

A room that is dedicated primarily to eating can make a big difference to your health, since it encourages people to eat together in an appropriate environment. People receive nourishment, not just from the food they eat, but from the company they share. It is also helpful for children as a suitable arena for learning basic table manners and social skills. Increasingly busy family schedules mean that it is no longer possible to share all meals, but try to have at least one meal a day together. If family members are older and have their own routines, making a daily meal out of the question, then aim for a family meal once a week. A dining room should be a relaxed environment that has a minimum of disturbance and interference from the television and work. Each meal should be seen as a special moment in the day, with the food enjoyed and appreciated, and the effort taken to cook it recognized. Here, also, the day's happenings can be discussed, shared, and enjoyed.

KEY

one Create a light, joyful, and happy environment in which to enjoy your food. A well-laid out table in this naturally lit room helps to ensure a positive eating experience. Keep the artificial lighting level low, but bright enough for people to see what they are eating.

two Candles and fresh flowers always help to make any meal special. Remember that you can easily change the mood by bringing in color. Red and orange are both warm, lively colors that stimulate

conversation, and you can introduce them in the candles or in fabrics such as a tablecloth or napkins.

three A familiar place to eat every day, which is always used for dining and not routinely taken over as a desk, helps to foster a healthy attitude towards food and eating.

four Choose a dining table that is of generous proportions, or that will easily extend to accommodate more people, so that you can invite friends to join you for a meal. The social exchanges that take place at

meal times are important for building healthy relationships, and sharing food with others deepens our connection with them. A wooden dining table is preferable to glass because it is distracting to be able to see through the surface. This can cause an uncomfortable sensation.

five Having bowls of fresh fruit, nuts or prepared raw vegetables readily available makes it easier for people to eat healthy in-between-meal snacks, rather than sweet cookies and cakes or salty processed foods.

six The natural wood chosen for the floor and table helps to create a relaxing environment.

seven Take a moment to express gratitude for the food you have in front of you. Even if you are not moved to say grace, a simple ritual of lighting a candle and having a moment of stillness helps to relax and prepare your body. Always thank the cook for the meal. It is helpful to eat at a regular time, as the body will get used to it and start to prepare itself in advance. It can be stressful not to know what time you will eat each evening.

THE HOME OFFICE: A CREATIVE
AND INSPIRING ENVIRONMENT

More people are choosing to work from home, to have the freedom of working for themselves, to enjoy greater flexibility, or to spend more time with their children. The working environment and amount of space will vary according to the type of work involved. Some will only require a desk, a phone and a shelf, while others will want a full-scale office with computers, printers, scanners, and perhaps even a resource library. While there are huge savings to be made by working from home, you must have to be prepared for the impact this lifestyle change can have on family life. After all, your home is your sanctuary away from the workplace. The first issue to consider is location. The best scenario is a separate building in the yard or in an extension. If that is impractical, try to take over a room near the front door if you will be having regular visitors, or choose a place that feels supportive to your kind of work, that has good natural light, and that is some distance away from your bedroom.

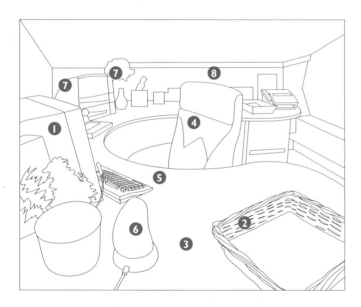

five Maintain a clear desk policy – clutter is stressful. Be selective about what paper you hold onto and what you decide to throw away.

six The salt crystal lamp helps to create more negative ions in the office environment. This serves to counteract the tiring atmosphere that results from positive ions generated by EMFs.

seven Plants are an essential part of an indoor environment. Apart from reconnecting people with the natural world, they are particularly helpful in rebalancing the atmosphere of an office area. Both the spider plant and the peace lily are on the NASA research list of plants that are good at removing indoor air pollutants. The latter is excellent at removing acetone, formaldehyde, and benzene. Put several plants near your printer, fax, and photocopier.

eight The physical stress caused by perceived pressure from the sloping ceiling can be mitigated by flooding that wall with light. Here two spotlights "lift" the wall, and using natural daylight bulbs makes it less tiring on the eyes.

KEY

one Computer monitors radiate harmful emissions so it is important to install a protection device. This one has Bioshield balls fitted. Anyone sitting here will not only be protected from the emissions, but will feel less drained after working at the computer over a period.

two Natural materials create a more relaxing and low-stress environment than one filled with man-made laminates. Whenever possible choose cane or wicker rather than PVC or plastics.

three Light wood is easy on the eye, making it a good material for a desk – black and white are more difficult for the eye to adjust to. Most desks have two elements, and are L-shaped to accommodate a computer on one side and a working area on the other. The curve on this desk is far more comfortable than having a square corner at the junction of the two work areas.

four Always make sure that you have a good chair with a high back to give support.

LEFT Avoid sitting under beams when working for a long time since they will cause unnecessary pressure on your body. Natural wood for the desk and flooring are ideal as they help to reduce stress by lowering dust and static levels. A key source of sickness in office buildings is the poor air quality. Toxins from equipment such as photocopiers and printers impregnate dust in the air, which is then charged up by electromagnetic radiation emanating from computers and other electrical equipment, and impedes breathing. When creating an office at home, make sure that you ventilate your space and keep the windows open. If your work involves talking on the phone, invest in a hands-free facility that will save you from crooking your neck to hold the phone. Prolonged cradling of the receiver can inflame tendons and cause back problems. If you are really going to enjoy the freedom of working from home, play classical music softly in the background. Baroque music has been found to be especially effective at synchronizing the two spheres of the brain, making you more creative and relaxed.

ABOVE LEFT Your work need not be too intrusive on family life. Computer equipment is getting smaller and smaller, and it is also possible to buy special desk furniture that allows you to slide your keyboard away when not in use. When you work from home you have more freedom to create a more inspiring environment that you might not otherwise have been able to achieve in a corporate office. Surround yourself with nature, flowers, and images that inspire you.

ABOVE This storage unit is perfect for hiding away all work-related equipment and is useful if your office has a combined function, such as a living or dining space. Shutting your work area away is also another practical way to create boundaries around your work and signal to yourself, as well as others, that the work day is over and you have "come home". Always choose an office chair rather than a dining chair because they are designed to give your back maximum support.

THE BEDROOM: A PERSONAL HAVEN

This is one of the most important rooms. A place where we spend around a third of our lives, it is an environment that should encourage deep, healing sleep. Choose neutral colors like white and cream or soft tones of pink, green, and blue to help to create a calm atmosphere. Keep clutter to a minimum so that the room is a tranquil refuge, and if the bedroom is used during the day, cover all signs of activity at night with screens. You could also change the lighting levels in the evening or use aromatherapy oils and music to remind yourself that the working day is over. Make sure there is nothing that will make a sound during the night, affecting the quality of your sleep. Above all, keep a watch on the chemicals you might have around – air fresheners, window or mirror cleaners, or furniture sprays. Investigate the new materials now available for bedding that deter dust-mites – their presence creates toxins that aggravate allergies, breathing problems, and irritable skin conditions.

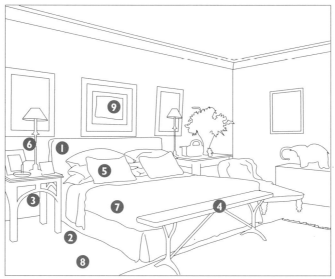

six Check the electromagnetic fields around your bed with a meter (see page 61). Avoid the use of clock radios that stay on all night and can interfere with the delicate electro-magnetic activity of your brain. Also, check the field of electrical cabling inside the walls behind the bed.

seven The quality of your mattress will affect the quality of your sleep. Never buy a secondhand mattress. Change your mattress at least every seven years and whenever you start a major new relationship. Explore the possibility of new magnetic pads that are now available to encourage a very deep level of sleep.

eight Soft, natural fiber rugs on wood floors are the best option in bedrooms. Reduce the influence of the outside world, and don't wear shoes in this room.

nine Choose images for the wall that are inspiring and have some personal meaning for you.

ten Open the windows every day to air it and keep the room fresh. Bring in plants for natural purification (see pages 96–98).

KEY

one Invest in a good bedhead, and place your bed against a solid wall for maximum protection and support. Make sure the bed has a good view of the door.

two Check to see if there are lines of geopathic stress running through your bedroom by dowsing (see pages 63–64). They are most harmful if you sleep over them. Move your bed away from the lines, and get someone to clear the negative energies, or buy equipment to harmonize them.

three Create a sense of balance for the occupants of a double bed by having balancing bedside tables or cabinets and lamps.

four A bed frame, chest, or appropriate piece of furniture (such as this bench) helps to contain the energy of the bed's occupants.

five Try to choose untreated cotton and linens for sheets and bedspreads. Man-made fibers amplify electro-magnetic fields, and formaldehyde emits from polycotton for years (see pages 56–60).

ABOVE Make sure that your curtains allow some daylight through in the morning. To be woken by the filtered morning light will support your biological clock in waking you naturally, instead of being jerked awake by an alarm clock in a pitch-black room. In an ideal world you would choose a smaller bedroom for sleeping and use a separate room as a dressing room for storing clothes, since this keeps the vibrations of the outside world away from your sleeping space. Always air any freshly dry-cleaned clothes before putting them back into the closet as they will release toxic chemicals. Do not put distracting entertainment equipment like music centers, televisions, and computers in your bedroom. Keep the rooms where family members sleep quiet and still, and convert one bedroom into a separate activity room for any computer games and children's toys. Never have a mirror or mirrored doors facing the bed, as they can cause restlessness or insomnia. If they cannot be removed, cover them at night.

ABOVE AND RIGHT Children's rooms need to sustain two functions – sleep and play – which require opposing supportive atmospheres. Sleep is more important, being fundamental to a child's development. Poor sleep can create hyperactivity, slow learning, and a poorer immune system. Soporific colors and gentle shades will calm a restless child, while orange, yellow and red will stimulate the mind, so these can be used in a play area. Avoid giving a child a television or computer in their own room since this will discourage them from interacting with other children, an important part of social development. Put bright colors, toys and high-tech equipment in a more social environment so the family can follow their different pursuits together. Televisions and computer screens put an unnecessarily high level of EMFs into a child's sleeping space, which affects their health. When redecorating, use organic materials so that you can use the room again as soon as possible. Don't put newborn babies into a newly decorated room immediately as they are very sensitive to chemicals, and exposure for 8–12 hours every day could overload their immune systems. Wooden floors also help to provide low allergy environments by creating less dust. Muslin cloth over a cot helps to contain a baby's sleeping space and is better than hanging mobiles over their heads.

THE BATHROOM: FOR CLEANSING AND RELAXATION

Nowadays, it is becoming more difficult to make time to attend to our physical needs. The bathroom should be a private refuge for cleansing, invigoration, contemplation, pampering and beautification, so make it healthy and reassuring. Water, the main element in the bathroom, has long been associated with purification and healing. However, it also conducts electromagnetic vibrations and dissolved chemicals, so check your water quality and install an appropriate filter. You should also check the electromagnetic fields radiating from the water supply. If the electrical wiring runs alongside highly conductive copper water pipes, EMFs will travel through your system, sapping your energy as you bathe. Read all product labels and only choose bathroom products with natural ingredients: chemicals in toiletries can be be neurotoxic, with the potential to disrupt brain and nerve functions, making you feel sluggish, depressed, and headachey (see pages 30–44).

KEY

one Mold can be especially harmful to people with respiratory problems, and it likes dark, damp places. Carpeting holds moisture that encourages mold, so choose wood or tiled floors. Instead of using spray mold cleaners that contain formaldehyde, use borax solution on tile grout and other bathroom surfaces.

two Make sure that as much light as possible can come in, and ventilate the room by keeping windows open or installing an extractor.

three Choose your bathroom furniture carefully – it should be made with natural materials like wood rather than synthetic products – and try to use towels made with untreated cotton.

four Avoid using glass for shelves as they are uncomfortable to be around when we are at our most vulnerable. Wood shelves are best.

five It is a good idea to have a shower at the end of the working day, as it will help to revitalize you by cleansing your body of the adverse effects of the harmful EMFs to which you are exposed during the day in most office environments.

six Soaking in a hot bath of Epsom salts and a handful of baking soda granules helps to detoxify the body. A daily sauna or session in a steam room can also be very helpful. Make sure that as well as a bright light for shaving, you also have a soft diffuse light (or candles) to increase the sense of relaxation when taking a leisurely bath.

seven The white color scheme makes the room feel fresh and clean. If pure white seems too clinical and unfriendly, it can be warmed up with pink or red towels, pictures, and plants.

eight It is a good idea to install a big mirror, since this will enable you to see your whole body. Avoid reflecting back a distorted or split image, such as one from a cabinet with a pair of mirrored doors.

nine Plants are great for bathrooms, and it is a good idea to choose those that love moisture. One plant is good, but a few more would be better.

ABOVE This cozy bathroom is compact and warm. It feels like an ideal place in which to relax because it has a simple, old-fashioned style and the colors of nature are well-represented. The chair and table make it feel inviting, and the mirror has a light above it to provide illumination.

The purpose of *The Healthy House Book* is to give you a simple model for understanding the effect of different sources of stress in our lives. It can't hope to answer all your questions, but the intention is to provide you with some guidance to start making different and better choices about how you live and work. Refer to the website www.thehealthyhome.com as a direct way of connecting you with hundreds of resources worldwide so that you can find the very latest information in the area that seems most relevant to you. When you have the knowledge you need, you can make different decisions about your health and feel more confident that the corrective action you are taking is the right one.

Where to begin

First, evaluate the health of your family. Who is unwell, how much energy do they have, what symptoms have they got?

Read the book again and check their symptoms or condition against those detailed in the different sections and see if there are any clues. This may lead you to tackle one particular area as a priority, or you may decide simply to take on each stressor one at a time and work with it. (See www.thehealthyhome.com for a handy questionnaire.)

Start by being positive

You may have found some of the information in this book rather surprising or even disturbing. In moving forward and deciding what to do next, the first thing to do is not to worry. When faced with fear, the Dalai Lama advises that you should focus the energy of your concern into finding out exactly what you can do, and then do it. If there is nothing you can do to solve the problem, then do not worry. Constant worry is an internal stressor that can be just as damaging as any of the other environmental stressors that have been discussed. Retain a positive outlook on life, and just do the best you can.

Focus on staying healthy

An ounce of prevention is worth a pound of cure. Don't wait until you get sick before making any changes. With so many people suffering from low energy and a whole range of energy-sapping conditions, most healthcare systems in the developed nations can no longer cope effectively. The solution lies with us taking personal responsibility for our own health.

The best way to do this is to take some preventative measures to stay well – especially since experts in preventative medicine estimate that 70 percent of diseases are preventable through a healthy diet. When the UK's Chief Medical Officer retired in September 1998, his final report recommended that it was pointless for the government to spend more money on health until people were willing to take responsibility for their own unhealthy lifestyles.

Take steps to protect yourself

We have to recognize that there are new threats to our health that we did not have before. Although we cannot see it, the energy field that surrounds us also needs protection. In the same way that we might wear protective clothing such as a cotton dust mask, rubber gloves, steel-capped boots, or a leather apron to do different tasks, we need to start using devices that protect our subtle energy fields. These are so crucial to our health, but they are constantly being attacked by invisible radiations and pollutants, at work as well as at home.

RIGHT Stressful situations, problems, hassles, and deadlines are often unavoidable, but they are much easier to manage if we can take ourselves away for a while to recharge. Make sure you take care of yourself. If you can't manage a walk in nature, then half an hour in your own personal retreat will help to restore equilibrium.

Be a more conscious consumer

Very few products carry information about the potential detrimental effect to our health. Now, with the worldwide web, we have access to an unprecedented amount of information. As a customer you can acquire much more knowledge so that you can make better choices on home purchases, and select ones that will have a more positive impact on family health.

So ask questions, read labels, buy less convenience products or appliances, reevaluate your need to buy, avoid using too many chemicals, eat organic foods, change your life, and see how your health improves. We can also recognize that everything we buy or do makes an impact – anything that harms the planet will also ultimately harm us. There is a cycle of connection where everything that goes around, does actually come around. Every new decision we make that improves our health and the quality of our home environment will also improve the quality of other peoples' lives. So strong is the connection, that everything we do in our own homes to change our lives will actually make a difference in the world.

Toxins in the body

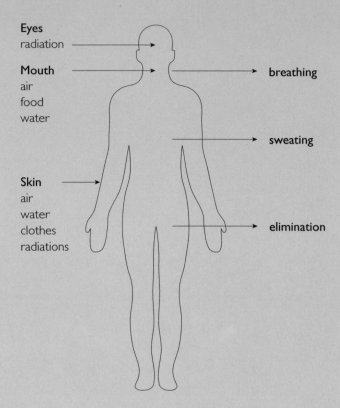

INPUT OF TOXINS
constantly increasing

OUTPUT OF TOXINS
needs to be increased

Eyes
radiation

Mouth
air
food
water

Skin
air
water
clothes
radiations

breathing

sweating

elimination

Toxins in the home

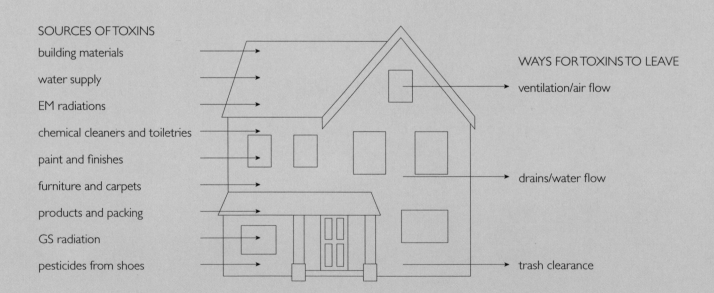

SOURCES OF TOXINS

building materials

water supply

EM radiations

chemical cleaners and toiletries

paint and finishes

furniture and carpets

products and packing

GS radiation

pesticides from shoes

WAYS FOR TOXINS TO LEAVE

ventilation/air flow

drains/water flow

trash clearance

Set high standards for your health

A survey by the Arthritis Foundation in the US in 2000 said that 89 percent of adults experience pain every month, but nearly two thirds will only see a doctor for help when they cannot stand it any longer. Many people in the survey (80 percent) believed that pains were just part of getting older. See pain and sickness as signs from your body that something about your lifestyle, diet, or environment doesn't suit you. Aim for vibrant health and energy, instead of settling for an absence of disease.

Find help and support

When you start making changes to your usual routines and purchases it can be rather daunting. Make contact with your local natural health food store if you don't already use one. They will give you plenty of guidance and can answer many questions. Read their noticeboard, buy health magazines, and get on the web. Visit a complementary health practitioner and ask for support with your lifestyle changes. Call in a professional to help you make changes in your home environment. Get to know your own needs by getting food sensitivity and allergy tests.

Children need special attention

Children are much more sensitive to environmental stresses, since harmful radiations and toxins have greater impact on their smaller, developing bodies. The nature of childhood is also changing dramatically. Previously engaged by active games and sports, now more of them entertain themselves with their own televisions, computers, and cellular phones.

A study of 1,300 German children published in June 2000 by Humboldt University in Berlin, concluded that youngsters from higher bracket income families were more likely to fall victim to allergies than those from lower income groups. This leads to a theory connected to the fact that the children of middle-class parents are brought up in immaculately clean homes, usually with access to computers, and also that they are less likely to play outside. This lifestyle means that they avoid exposure to germs that help to develop resistance and strengthen immune function, putting themselves more at risk of asthma and eczema.

ABOVE The two most important aspects of living a healthy life are a good diet and good quality sleep. Ensure that your bedroom is providing you with the perfect environment for deep, restful sleep: simple low-allergy surroundings, natural materials, no electromagnetic radiation, and an absence of geopathic stress.

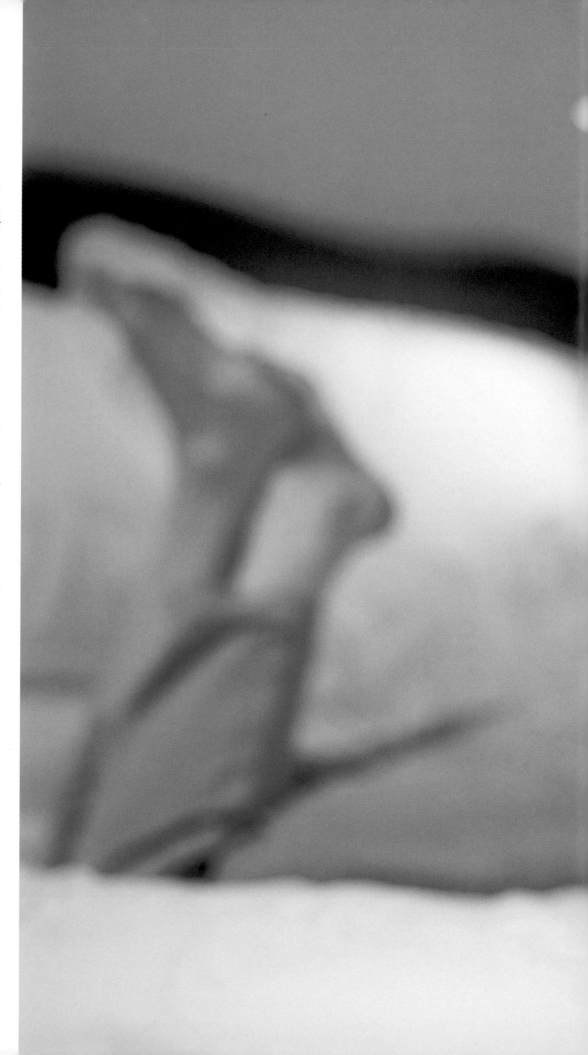

Prepare for a long old age

Life expectancy is continually lengthening and has doubled in the last 50 years. If health experts maintain that we can control 40 percent of those elements that affect longevity, then our life truly is in our hands. And if our retirement is no longer about resting but more like the beginning of another exciting chapter, we need to make sure that we have the physical fitness, mental clarity, energy, and flexibility to enjoy it.

Mind, body, and spirit, too

In taking more care of ourselves, we need to remember that our spiritual nature needs nourishment as well. An American psychologist who surveyed 126,000 people found that those who attended their church (or other place of worship) were more than 30 percent more likely to live longer. However we decide to reconnect with our spiritual life, our quest for it will make a huge difference, not only to our own personal health, but also to the health of humanity and the earth.

RIGHT Life is too short not to find some way of being happy. Reduce your personal stress, review your working hours, change your routine, and improve the quality of your home and health. Do whatever you need to, so that you can enjoy every day as it comes. A happy and optimistic attitude will help you to enjoy life to the full and live longer.

WEBSITE

www.thehealthyhome.com
The website has a full listing of international contacts and resources. Check our pages entitled Frequently Asked Questions.

RESOURCES

Gina Lazenby can be contacted at:
The Healthy Home, PO Box 249,
Keighley, Yorkshire, BD20 8YN
Gina@thehealthyhome.com
Information on The Healthy Home: tel: 07000 336474
(+44 7000 336474)

info@thehealthyhome.com
Holds a register of professional feng shui practitioners, dowsers, home harmonizers, and specialists who can evaluate electromagetic field problems. There is also a catalog of products and details of courses, workshops, and talks, which cover many of the topics in this book.

A Resource Pack with suppliers, professionals, and stocked products is available by mail. Please send a stamped, addressed envelope to the above address.

FURTHER READING

For practical support in clutter clearing
Clear your Clutter with Feng Shui, Karen Kingston (Piatkus Books, 1998)
Clear your Desk, Declan Treacy (Century, 1991)
Clutter's Last Stand, Don Aslett (Writer's Digest Books, 1984)
Downshifters: The Guide to Happiness and Simpler Living, Polly Ghazi and Judy Jones (Coronet, 1997)
How to Conquer Clutter, Stephanie Culp (Writer's Digest Books, 1990)
Simplicity, Elaine St. James (Thorsons, 1997)
Voluntary Simplicity, Duane Elgin (Quill, 1981)

Towards a more natural way of living
Eco Friendly House Plants, BC Wolverton (Phoenix, 1997)
The Green Home, Karen Christensen (Piatkus, 1995)
Healing Environments, Carol Venolia (Celestial Books, 1988)
The Healing Home, Suzy Chiazzari (Ebury Press, 1998)
Heart and Home, Beverly Pagram (Gaia, 1997)
The Holistic Home, Joanna Trevelyan (Apple, 1998)
Home Safe Home, Debra Lynn (Putnam Publishing Group, 1997)
Natural Housekeeping, Beverly Pagram (Gaia, 1997)
Places of the Soul, Christopher Day (Aquarian, 1990)
The Power of Place, Winifred Gallagher (Harper Perennial, 1994)
The Spirit of the Home, Jane Alexander (Thorsons, 1999)

Towards a more natural way of building
The Healthy House, Sydney and Joan Baggs (Thames and Hudson, 1996)
The Natural House Book, David Pearson (Conran Octopus, 1992)
Natural House Catalog, David Press (Fireside, 1996)
Places of the Soul, Christopher Day (Aquarian, 1990)
The Timeless Way of Building, Christopher Alexander (Oxford University Press, 1979)
The Whole House Book, Pat Borer and Cindy Harris (New Futures, 1998)

Learning more about cleansing homes
Creating Sacred Space with Feng Shui, Karen Kingston (Piatkus, 1996)
Sacred Space, Denis Linn (Rider, 1995)
The Smudge Pack, Jane Alexander (Thorsons, 1999)

Reconnecting with ancient wisdom
Feng Shui for the Soul, Denise Linn (Rider, 1999)
The Feng Shui House Book, Gina Lazenby (Conran Octopus, 1999)
Feng Shui Made Easy, William Spear (Thorsons, 1995)
Home Design from Inside Out, Robin Lennon (Penguin, 1997)
Simple Feng Shui, Gina Lazenby (Conran Octopus, 1999)

Learning more about harmful energies
Electromagnetic Pollution Solutions, Dr. Glen Swatwout (AERAI Publishing, 1991)
H is for Ecohome, Anna Kruger (Gaia Books, 1991)
Handbook of Biological Effects of Electromagnetic Fields, C. Plk & E. Poston (CRC Press, 1995)
The Healthy Home, Linda Mason Hunter (Pocket Books, 1989)
Home Safe Home, Debra Linn Dodd (Tarcher Putnam, 1997)
It's so Natural, Alan Hayes (Gill & Macmillan, 1998)
Killing Fields in the Home, Alastair Philips (Green Audit, 1999)
Living with Electricity, Alistair Philips (Powerwatch, 1997)
Safe as Houses, D. Cowan and Rodney Girdlestone (Gateway Books, 1996)
Water Electricity and Health, Alan Hall (Hawthorn Press, 1997)

For a further understanding of earth energies and dowsing
Geopathic Stress, Jane Thurnell (Element Books, 1995)
The Pendulum Kit, Sig Longren (Simon & Schuster, 1990)
Spiritual Dowsing, Sig Lonegren (Gothic Imaging Publishing, 1986)

Improving your health and energy
Ageless Body, Timeless Mind, Deepak Chopra (Rider, 1998)
The Book of Macrobiotics, Michio Kushi (Japan Publications, 1987)
The Changing Seasons Macrobiotic Cookbook, Aveline Kushi (Avery Publishing Group, 1985)
The Creation of Health, Caroline Myss & C. Norman Shealy (Bantam, 1999)
Diet for a New World, John Robbins (Avon Books, 1992)
Discovery of Magnetic Health, George Washnis (Health Research, 1998)
Electrohealing, Roger Coghill (Thorsons, 1992)
Food and Healing, Ann-Marie Colbin (Ballantime, 1986)
Forever Young, Marisa Peer (Michael Joseph, 1997)
The Organic Director, Clive Litchfield (Green Books, 2000)
The Promise of Sleep, William Dement (Delacorbe Press, 1999)
Psychic Protection, William Bloom (Piatkus, 1996)
Reverse Aging, Sang Whang (Siloam Enterprise, 1990)
The Self-Healing Cookbook, Kristina Turner (Earthtones Press, 1987)
Spontaneous Healing, Dr. Andrew Weil (Little Brown & Co, 1995)
Sugar Blues, William Duffy (Warner Books, 1975)
Supertherapies, Jane Alexander (Bantam, 1996)
Your Face Never Lies, Michio Kushi (Avery Publishing Group, 1983)
10 Day Rebalance Program, Jon Sandifer (Rider, 1998)
8 Weeks to Optimum Health, Dr. Andrew Weil (Warner Books, 1997)

For an understanding of color
Color with Healing, Theo Gimbel (Gaia, 1994)
Color Healing, Lilian Verner-Bondsa (Lorenz Books, 1999)

For de-stressing
The Book of Calm, Paul Wilson (Penguin, 1999)
Laughter the Best Medicine, Robert Holden (Thorsons, 1993)
Stress: 101 Strategies for Stress Survival, Robert Holden (Thorsons, 1992)

For regaining a sense of balance in your life
Feng Shui Food, Steven Saunders and Simon Brown (The Lyons Press, 2000)
Hungry Spirit, Charles Handy (Arrow Books, 1998)
The Life Balance Program, Peta Lyn Farwagi (Orion, 1998)
The Reinvention of Work, Mathew Fox (HarperCollins, 1994)
Successful but Something Missing, Ben Renshaw (Rider, 2000)
The Work We Were Born To Do, Nigel Williams (Element, 1999)
Your Money or Your Life, Joe Dominguez & Vicki Robin (Penguin, 1993)

INDEX

fireplaces 130
flea collars 36
floorcoverings 35, 39
floors 34, 130, 133, 135, 139, 143, 146, 148
flowers 130, 135, 139
fluorescent lighting 59–60, 135
fluoridated water 41–3
food 11, 74, 31, 36, 77, 86–8, 135, 137, 139, 150, 153
formaldehyde 34–5, 40, 41, 98, 132, 140, 148
Framlington Heart Study 87
front doors 47–9
full spectrum lights 60
furnishings 11, 31, 35
furniture 41, 50

G

garlic 87
gas 33, 36–7, 137
gasoline 33, 35
geopathic stress 61–5
Globe, The 67
glue 35, 39
gold 114
golf courses 36
Grant, Dr. William 77
green 119, 145
gynecological problems 77

H

hair dryers 22, 25
hallways 16, 47
halogen lights 60
headaches 28, 31, 33, 37, 39, 40, 43, 46, 59, 63, 77, 87, 148
health, taking responsibility for 150–4
heart attacks 11, 74, 83, 87, 91
Helios 1 63
herbicides 41, 43
Hertl, Dr. Hans 77
home harmonizing 19, 106–11
home improvement products 31, 34–5
home maintenance 19, 46–7, 63
home toxins 33
hormones 22
household cleaners 11, 33, 42, 43–5, 135, 145
Hunter, Lynda Mason (*Healthy Home*) 33
hyperactivity 60, 146
hypertension 74

I

immune system 21, 22, 28, 62, 66–7, 69, 87, 92, 102, 146
inattentiveness 31
incandescent light bulbs 59, 135
incense 106
insecticides 31, 34
insoles, magnetic 25, 28, 102
insomnia 31
insulation 8, 31, 34
International Commission on Non-ionising Radiation Protection 25
internet 150, 153
ions 37, 39, 59, 140
irritability 40, 59
isocyanates 34

J

Japan 88, 102–4
joint pain 40, 116
jute 39

K

Kearns, Linda 88
kerosene 40
kitchens 134–7
knives 135
Kruger, Anna (*H is for Ecohome*) 40
Kushi, Aveline (*The Changing Seasons*) 135

L

lead 33
lethargy 37, 39, 55, 63, 83, 92, 148
leukaemia 22
libido 27
lifestyle stress 66
lighting 56–60, 130, 133, 135, 139, 140, 145
linoleum 39
living rooms 130–3
London Hazard Centre 60

M

magnetism, Earth's 21, 22–5, 102–5
mattresses 145
measuring EMFs 25, 28–9, 145
meat 74, 87
meditation 94
medium density fiberboard (MDF) 34–5, 41, 133
melatonin 22
memory loss 39, 41
menopause 88

microwaves 21, 22, 77, 137
migraine 63
mirroring 46–7
mirrors 49, 146, 148
miscarriage 27, 60
mixing energies 53
moods 55–6
mothballs 36
mold 148
muscle pain 40, 116
myalgesic encephalomyelitis (ME) 22, 43
Myss, Caroline (*The Creation of Health*) 69

N

National Research Council 31
natural cleaners 43–5, 135
natural light 21, 36, 55–7, 97, 98, 105, 130, 133, 135, 139, 146, 148
nature 96–8
nausea 35, 37, 39, 40, 43
negative ions 37
nervous disorders 31
New England Journal of Medicine 75
nitrogen dioxide 37

O

oatmeal 123
office buildings 55
offices, home 53, 140–3
orange 120, 130, 139, 146
organic food 11, 31, 36, 77, 87, 150, 153
osteoporosis 77
Ott, Dr. John 56, 60, 105
over-eating 74

P

packaging 31, 35
pads, magnetic 104, 145
paints 31, 33, 39–40, 146
paper clutter 16, 140
Parkinson's disease 31
Pearson, David (*The Natural House Catalog*) 39
perfumes 33
pesticides 11, 31, 33, 36, 39, 41, 43, 77, 87
petrochemicals 31, 40
phenol 39
Philips, Alasdair 21
Philpott, Dr. William H. 102
pictures 130, 143, 145, 148
pineal gland 21
pink 114, 145

ACKNOWLEDGMENTS

The publisher would like to thank the following photographers and agencies for their kind permission to reproduce the photographs in this book.

2 Ray Main/Mainstream; **3** Abode UK; **5** above left Michael Busselle; **5** above right Simon Brown/The Interior Archive; **5** center left Alexander van Berge; **5** center right Jacqui Hurst; **5** below left Ingalill Snitt; **5** below right F.Lemarchand/ Marie France; **6** Alexander van Berge; **10** Abode UK; **12** Simon Upton/The Interior Archive; **14** Deidi von Schaewen; **15** left Andrew Wood/The Interior Archive; **15** right Camera Press; **16** left Lizzie Orme/ Robert Harding; **16** right Sandra Lane/Robert Harding; **17** Gloria Nicol/ Robert Harding; **18** Ray Main/ Mainstream; **19** left Earl Carter/Belle/Arcaid/(Designer Christian Liaigre); **19** right Laurence Dutler/Getty Images; **20** J.C.N'Diaye/Camera Press; **21** Ray Main/Mainstream; **22** M.Vanmoerkerke/Verne Fotografie; **23** Ray Main/ Mainstream; **24** Andrew Wood/The Interior Archive/ (Designer Peter Wylly/Babylon Design.); **26** Tim Beddow/ The Interior Archive/(Designer Melissa Stevenson); **27** left Peter Poulides/Getty Images; **27** right Dennis O'Clair/ Getty Images; **30** Paul Ryan/International Interiors/(Designer Francine Gardiner); **32** Ingalill Snitt; **34** Paul Ryan/International Interiors/(Designer G.Pensoy); **35** left Fritz von der Schulenburg/The Interior Archive/ (Designer John Stefaridis); **35** right Paul Ryan/International Interiors; **36** Paul Ryan/International Interiors/(Designer Caroline Breef); **37** Ray Main/Mainstream; **38** left Simon Brown/ The Interior Archive; **39** left Jacques Dirand/The Interior Archive/(Owner Gerard Decooter); **39** right Deidi von Schaewen; **40** Fritz von der Schulenburg/The Interior Archive/(Owner Joanne Crevelung; **41** Ingalill Snitt; **42** left Jacqui Hurst; **42** right Morel M.Pierre/Marie Claire Maison/(Stylist Daniel Rozensztroch); **44** Luc de Champris/ Marie France/(Stylist M.Boquillon); **45** Jacqui Hurst; **46** F.Le Marchand/Marie France (Designer Armand Ventilo); **47** Paul Ryan/ International Interiors/(Designer Kristina Ratia); **48** Tim Beddow/The Interior Archive/(Designer Kathryn Ireland); **50** above Paul Ryan(MC2 Design) /International Interiors; **50** below Tim Beddow/The Interior Archive/(Designer Colin Childerley); **51** Camera Press/ (Conran/Willcocks Home.); **52** Paul Ryan/International Interiors/(Architect Jacob Crunstedt); **53** Deidi von Schaewen; **54** Abode UK; **55** Paul Ryan/International Interiors/(Designer Christian Liaigre); **56** Paul Ryan/ International Interiors/ (Designer Francine Gardiner); **57** Deidi von Schaewen; **58–59** Fritz von der Schulenburg/ (Architect Nico Rensch)/The Interior Archive; **61** left Simon Upton/The Interior Archive; **61** right Simon Upton/The Interior Archive; **62** left Brian Carter/The Garden Picture Library; **62** right Jerry Pavia/The Garden Picture Library; **66–67** Frank Herholdt/Getty Images; **67** David Harding/ GettyOne Stone; **68** left Tim Beddow/The Interior Archive (Designer Marie France Brown); **68** right Merel M.Pierre/ Marie Claire Maison; **72–73** main picture Tim Beddow/The Interior Archive; **75** Joff Lee/Anthony Blake Library; **76** Joff Lee/Anthony Blake Library; **78** Michelle Garrett/Insight Photo Library; **81** Tim Beddow/The Interior Archive.; **82** Michelle Garrett/Insight Photo Library; **83** above Ray Main/ Mainstream; **83** below Insight Photo Library; **84** Tim Beddow/The Interior Archive; **85** Paul Ryan/International Interiors (Designer Mary Foley); **86** main picture Suki Coughlin/Camera Press; **87** Michele Garrett/Robert Harding; **88** Andrew Wood/The Interior Archive; **89** Tim Imrie/ Anthony Blake Library; **90–91** Caroline Penn/ IMPACT; **93** left Carol Ford/Getty Images; **93** right Phillip Condit/Getty Images; **94** James Darell/Getty Images; **95** Edina van der Wyck/The Interior Archive; **96** Jane Legate/ The Garden Picture Library; **97** Mayer-Le Scanff/The Garden Picture Library; **99** Tim Beddow/The Interior Archive; **100–101** Camera Press/(Conran/Willcocks Home.); **102** John Lund/ Getty Images; **103** NASA/ K.Horgan/Getty Images; **104** Paul Grebliunas/Getty Images; **106** Fair Lady/Camera Press; **107** Fritz von der Schulenburg/The Interior Archive; **113** left Tosi Nicholas/ Marie Claire Maison; **113** right Simon Brown/The Interior Archive.; **114** Gilles de Chabaneix/Marie Claire Maison/ (Owner Jenny Jackson); **115** Simon Brown/ The Interior Archive; **116** left Christopher Drawe/Robert Harding/ (IPC Magazines Ltd.);**116–117** Fritz von der Schulenburg/ The Interior Archive; **118** Fritz von der Schulenburg/The Interior Archive; **119** Paul Ryan/ International Interiors (Designer Sharone Einhorn); **120** Jacques Dirand/The Interior Archive; **121** left Simon Mc Bride/The Interior Archive; **121** right Dominic Blackmore/ Robert Harding/IPC Syndication; **122** Tim Beddow/The Interior Archive; **123** Andrew Wood/The Interior Archive; **124** left Cecilia Innes/The Interior Archive; **124–125** Ray Main/Mainstream; **126–127** Morin Ardoui/ Marie Claire Maison; **128** Alexander van Berge; **130–131** Tim Beddow/ Interior Archive (Artist: Martin Mooney); **132–133** Henry Wilson/The Interior Archive/ (Designer Roger Lockhardt); **133** left Richard Felber; **133** right Paul Ryan/International Interiors/(Owners Kristina and Bjorn Sahlquist); **134–135** Paul Ryan/International Interiors/ (Designer Gennifer Houser); **136** Ray Main/ Mainstream; **137** Deidi von Schaewen; **138–139** Tim Beddow/The Interior Archive/ (Artist Martin Mooney); **140–141** Harry Archer/Viewpoint; **142** Andrew Wood/The Interior Archive/(Owner Mandy Oakley); **143** left Richard Felber; **143** right Russel Sadur/ Inspirations/ Robert Harding; **144–145** Tim Beddow/The Interior Archive/(Designer Karen Newman); **146** left Fritz von der Schulenburg/The Interior Archive/(Designer Mimi O'Connell); **146** right Dominic Blackmore/Homes and Ideas/IPC Syndication; **147** Mads Mogensen; **148–149** Tim Beddow/The Interior Archive; **149** right Elizabeth Whiting & Associates; **151** Paul Ryan/International Interiors (Designer Sharone Einhorn); **153–155** Ray Main/Mainstream.

Every effort has been made to trace the copyright holders and we apologize in advance for any unintentional omission and would be pleased to insert the appropriate acknowledgement in any subsequent edition.

Author acknowledgments

First of all a big thank you to my partner, Morel Fourman, for without his insights and the journey we have taken together in creating our own healthy home, this book really would not have come about. I also have enormous gratitude for the support of my editor, Emma Clegg, who had the patience of a saint and to whom I apologize for causing so many headaches as deadlines slipped and schedules had to be reorganized. I am also very grateful to the many others in the team at Conran Octopus who were involved at some stage on the book, including Mary Lambert, Lucy Holmes, Isobel de Cordova, Julia Pashley, Lucy Nicholson, Lara McCann, and Kate Haxell. Thanks also to Susannah Gough for helping to get the ball rolling in the first place.

As with any huge project there are many people along the way who give support, offer encouragement, or make some kind of input that adds value to the end result. Forgive me if you are not all included here, but you each have my heartfelt thanks for being there when needed. I would particularly like to thank Ellie Baker for demonstrating the home harmonizing techniques in the photography so beautifully. Also to Alasdair and Jean Philips of Powerwatch, Frans Van Til, Antonia Chavasse, Robert Borruso at Construction Resources, Jon Sandifer, Jan Cisek, Pat Duggan, Ann Currie, Janette Crabtree, Rolf Gordon, Catherine McNaughton, Jules Klapper, and John Jukes who have all made their contribution in some way to the accuracy or content of this book. With particular thanks, too, to Perspective Scientific Limited (tel: 020 7486 6837; fax: 020 7487 3023; service@perspective.co.uk; www.perspective.co.uk), who provided us with a hand-held radiation monitor for photography.

Thanks to Joan Spear for her cheerleading encouragement, and to my family who I am sure would have liked to have seen a bit more of me during this writing episode but were very understanding. I would also like to thank Nellie, whose nutritional advice made a big impact on my life, as well as Keith Ashton, Borut Lovrecic, and Anthony Robbins. My thanks to the teachers who were part of the Feng Shui Network International education program and shared so much of their knowledge about health, especially William Spear, Roger Green, Bob Longacre, David Pearson, Jeannie Towers, Karen Kingston, Roger Coghill, Richard Creightmore, and also to the many students and graduates who were involved in our program. Thank you to those who participated in the Home Harmoniser training program, especially Denise Linn for supporting me with the original vision, and Faith Tame and Davina Shadwick, who helped make it happen, and also to the many people who were interested enough to attend my Healthy Home courses. And finally, I would like to express my gratitude to the authors, publishers, researchers, and teachers who are committed to providing information, education, and resources so that we can all make this a healthier world, with special thanks to Caroline Myss, Dr. Norman Shealy, Lynn McTaggart, Carol Venolia, Debra Lynn Dadd, Jacques Surbeck, Dr. Hans Hertl, Michio and Aveline Kushi, and Dr. Andrew Weil.